CDs, Super Glue, and Salsa

series 3

HOW EVERYDAY PRODUCTS ARE MADE

CDs,
Super Glue, and Salsa

series **3**

HOW EVERYDAY PRODUCTS ARE MADE

Volume 1: A-G

Mei Ling Rein, Editor

Allison McNeill, Project Editor

Detroit • New York • San Diego • San Francisco • Cleveland • New Haven, Conn. • Waterville, Maine • London • Munich

THOMSON
GALE

CDs, Super Glue, and Salsa, Series 3

Mei Ling Rein, Editor

Project Editor
Allison McNeill

Permissions
Margaret Chamberlain

Imaging and Multimedia
Dean Dauphinais, Christine O'Bryan, Dan Newell

Product Design
Mark Howell, Cynthia Baldwin

Composition
Evi Seoud

Manufacturing
Rita Wimberley

For other books on the subject(s) discussed in this book, look in the card catalog, under the checked headings:

LIBRARY OF CONGRESS CATALOGING-IN-PUBLICATION DATA

CD's, super glue, and salsa : how everyday products are made: series 3 / Mei Ling Rein, editor.

   p. cm.

   Summary: Thirty entries describe the history and manufacturing process of such products as M&M's, spacesuits, and air conditioners, including their design, raw materials, quality control, and future enhancements.

   Includes bibliographical references and index.

   ISBN 0-7876-6476-6 (set) – ISBN 0-7876-6477-4 (v. 1) – ISBN 0-7876-6478-2 (v. 2)
✓ 1. Manufactures–History–Juvenile literature. [1. Manufactures.] I. Rein, Mei Ling.

TS146.C37 2002
670–dc21   2002011307

Printed in the United States of America
10 9 8 7 6 5 4 3 2 1

Contents

Reader's Guide

CDs, Super Glue, and Salsa: How Everyday Products Are Made, Series 3, answers all the questions about the manufacturing of thirty products students use, see, hear about, or read about every day. From common items like ballpoint pens and DVD players, to the less-common, like gas masks and spacesuits, entries describe in vivid detail the whys and hows of the inventions, provide step-by-step descriptions of the manufacturing processes, and even offer predictions about product enhancements for the future.

CDs, Super Glue, and Salsa's photos, illustrations, and lively, fun-to-read language make it easy to understand the sometimes complicated processes involved in creating these everyday products. Use Series 3 along with Series 1 and Series 2 for a one-stop guide to the details behind ninety of today's most fascinating products.

Format

CDs, Super Glue, and Salsa entries are arranged alphabetically across two volumes. In each entry, students will learn the secrets behind the manufacture of a product through the details of its history, including who invented it and why; how it was developed and how it works; how and from what it is made; how the product might be used in the future; and a list of books, periodicals, and Web sites that offer additional information.

Entry subheads make it easy for students to scan entries for just the information they need. Entries include sections that feature the following information:

- Background of product, including details on its history or development
- Raw materials needed for production
- Design of product and how it works
- Manufacturing process
- Quality control
- Future products
- For More Information

Additional Features

The many sidebars present entertaining and interesting facts that pertain to each product. A glossary of product-specific terms runs in the margin of each entry defining difficult terms. The uses and manufacturing processes of each product are enlivened with ninety-four photos and fifty-five illustrations. Each volume includes a general subject index, including entries from Series 1 and Series 2, that provides easy access to entries by listing important terms, processes, materials, and people.

Comments and Suggestions

We welcome comments on this work as well as suggestions for other products to be featured in future editions of *CDs, Super Glue, and Salsa.* Please write: Editors, *CDs, Super Glue, and Salsa,* U•X•L, 27500 Drake Road, Farmington Hills, Michigan, 48331-3535; call toll-free: 1-800-877-4253; fax to 248-699-8097; or send e-mail via http://www.gale.com.

Air Conditioner

An air conditioner is a group of equipment that "conditions" the air by controlling not only the temperature but also the humidity (moisture level), circulation, and purity of the air within a room or a building. It usually consists of a pump called a compressor, a condenser, an evaporator, and a refrigerant (see below). Most people associate air conditioning with cooling the air during warm weather. However, air conditioning also involves heating the air during cold weather. In both cases, air conditioning provides human comfort.

An air conditioner not only controls the temperature, it also regulates the humidity, circulation, and purity of the air within a room or a building.

The cooling capacity, or size, of an air conditioner is rated by the number of British thermal units (Btu) of heat it can remove per hour. Btu is the amount of heat required to raise the temperature of one pound (0.45 kilogram) of water one degree Fahrenheit (0.56 degree Celsius) per hour. Air conditioner sellers and contractors help consumers determine the size of the air conditioner unit needed using published calculation procedures recommended by industry experts.

Keeping cool through the ages

Since early times, people have looked for ways to keep cool. Ancient Greeks and Romans built public baths, which were community facilities that accommodated hundreds of people. Some people cooled the air entering their homes by hanging wet grass mats over windows and doors. Others used big leaves to fan themselves.

The powerful and wealthy beat the heat in different ways. Roman emperors reportedly ordered mountain snow transported to their palaces during the summer months. Some people had their servants pack snow between the walls of their homes. Still others had slaves fanning blocks of ice. Around 1500, Leonardo da Vinci (1452–1519), noted for his many clever inventions, constructed a mechanical fan to circulate the air in the home of a duchess.

The first air conditioners

The first attempts to condition air within enclosed spaces occurred during the eighteenth and nineteenth centuries. The purpose of the air conditioning was not to cool people but to provide humidity in textile factories so that fabric thread would not break due to the dry air. Water sprays and pots of hot water were used to keep the air moist. In 1842, American doctor John Gorie (1803–1855), having invented mechanical refrigeration, applied the same principle to cool patients' rooms. In 1902, the first air conditioner designed for human comfort was installed at the New York Stock Exchange. The term "air conditioning" was coined in 1906 by textile engineer Stuart Cramer (1868–1940), who invented a device to freshen and humidify his textile factory by adding moisture to the surroundings.

Father of air conditioning

Mechanical engineer Willis Carrier (1876–1950) is credited for developing the formulas that form the basis for the air conditioning system. He first created an air conditioner for a printing factory in Brooklyn, New York, in 1902. Fluctuating temperature and humidity caused changes in paper size so that the colored inks did not line up properly during printing. Carrier solved the problem by devising two sets of cooling coils (groups of tubes) over which he passed the air during hot weather. During cold weather, he piped in steam from the factory boilers. By 1907, Carrier's air conditioning system had been installed in several textile factories, a shoe factory, and a drug company.

In 1921, Carrier invented the centrifugal refrigeration machine, which enabled the air conditioning of large areas. While industries were the first to use Carrier's machine, commercial buildings, including department stores, hotels, and movie theaters, soon followed. In 1930, the White House became air conditioned. Although Carrier introduced the residen-

---

compressor: The part of the air conditioner that pumps the refrigerant through the system.

condenser: The part of the air conditioner that removes heat from the refrigerant and helps transfer that heat to the outside.

conductor: A material that lets heat pass through it.

corrosion: The slow wearing away of a metal by a liquid or a gas. For example, rusting of iron can result from exposure to moisture.

evaporator: The part of the air conditioner through which a refrigerant vapor flows, absorbing heat and cooling the surrounding air.

fins: Thin aluminum strips on the outer surface of an evaporator or condenser, enhancing the transfer of heat.

The air conditioner condenser, usually located outside of the home, helps fight off the heat on a hot summer's day. *Photograph by Kelly A. Quin. Copyright © Kelly A. Quin. Reproduced by permission of the photographer.*

tial air conditioner called the "Weathermaker" in 1928, it was not until the end of World War II (1939–45) that it was installed in American homes.

Raw Materials

Air conditioners are made of different types of metal, including copper and aluminum. Plastic, which is lightweight and inexpensive, may also be used. Copper and aluminum are important raw materials in many air conditioning components (parts), because they are good heat conduc-

galvanized steel: Steel that is coated with a thin layer of zinc to protect against corrosion.

refrigerant: The working fluid that circulates through the air conditioning system, absorbing heat indoors and discarding it outdoors.

stainless steel: Steel that does not rust.

tors, contributing to the efficiency of the system. In addition, these two metals can be easily shaped and bent and are resistant to corrosion (the slow wearing out of a metal by a liquid or a gas). Aluminum's light weight is an additional benefit.

Other air conditioner components are made of stainless steel, which is also resistant to rusting and other environmental changes. Self-contained units that house the refrigeration system are usually encased in sheet metal, produced by flattening steel with rollers. The sheet metal is covered with a powder coating to protect it from environmental conditions.

The refrigerant is the working fluid that circulates through the air conditioning system. Refrigerants used include hydrocarbons, ammonia, and water. Hydrochlorofluorocarbon (HCFC), which goes by the trade name R-22, is the refrigerant most commonly used in air conditioners. However, its global manufacture is being phased out (reduced in stages over a period of time) because of its negative effect on the ozone layer (oxygen layer that protects the earth from harmful ultraviolet rays). Scientists are researching suitable replacements for HCFCs. New air conditioners that are being manufactured use a chlorine-free refrigerant called Puron®, or R-410A.

Design

An air conditioner has four basic parts—a pump called the compressor, an evaporator, a condenser, and an expansion valve. It also contains a refrigerant, or a working fluid, that continuously moves through the air conditioning system. Most residential air conditioners get their power from a combination of an electric motor and pump. Some may use a gas engine and a pump.

The process of air conditioning involves the drawing in of heat from the air inside the home and then releasing that heat outdoors. These functions are performed by the refrigerant as it circulates through the air conditioning system. The pump is designed to increase system pressure and circulate the refrigerant.

The refrigerant, in the form of a low-pressure vapor (gas), starts at the compressor, in which it is "compressed," or squeezed, changing into a hot,

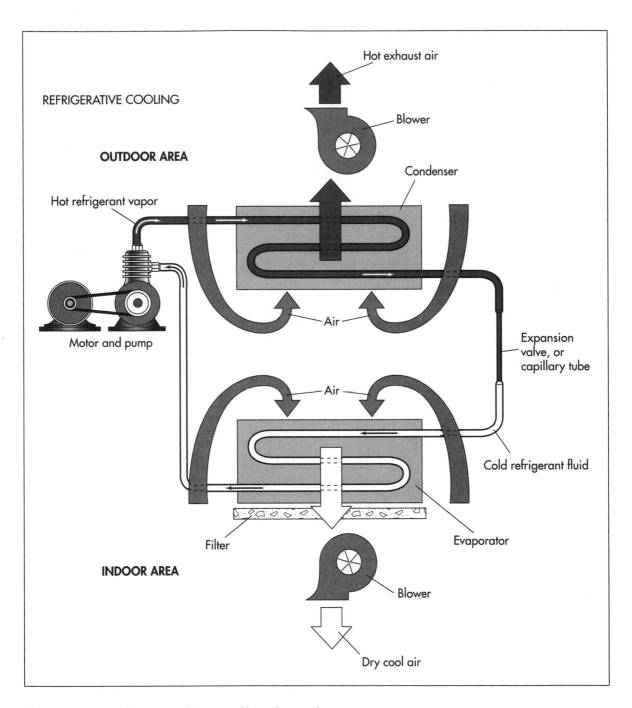

REFRIGERATIVE COOLING

Hot exhaust air

Blower

OUTDOOR AREA

Condenser

Hot refrigerant vapor

Motor and pump

Air

Expansion valve, or capillary tube

Air

Cold refrigerant fluid

Filter

Evaporator

INDOOR AREA

Blower

Dry cool air

The components of an air conditioner and how they work.

high-pressure vapor. The hot refrigerant vapor travels through a condenser coil, which has metal fins all around it. The fins help the refrigerant transfer heat to the outside, causing the refrigerant to change to a liquid.

Next, the liquid refrigerant flows into the evaporator through a narrow expansion valve called a capillary tube. The capillary tube allows the refrigerant's pressure to drop, causing it to evaporate. In the meantime, the hot air in the room is drawn to the evaporator surface through its metal fins. The refrigerant circulating in the evaporator coil absorbs that heat and thus cools the room. In the process, the refrigerant changes into a low-pressure vapor, returns to the compressor, and restarts its circulation through the air conditioning system.

The Manufacturing Process

Most air conditioners start out as sheet metal and structural steel shapes. A sheet metal is usually steel and is made by pressing the metal under pressure between rollers. A structural steel shape is a basic construction material. It is a very strong steel that has been shaped.

Constructing the casing, brackets, and other supports

1 The casing that houses the air conditioner unit is made of sheet metal. The sheet metal has usually been galvanized, or coated with a thin layer of zinc to protect it against corrosion. The galvanized sheet metal is also used to form the bottom pan, face plates, and various support brackets. A shear press, a machine that cuts by using a mold and applying pressure, is used to cut the different air conditioner parts.

Structural steel shapes are used to make some of the brackets and supports. The steel shapes are cut and mitered. Mitering refers to the process of forming a perpendicular joint, usually at a 45-degree angle, so that it could be attached to a similar piece to form a 90-degree corner.

Punch pressing the sheet metal forms

2 From the shear press, the sheet metal is loaded on a CNC (Computer Numerical Control) punch press, which uses two matching dies, or molds, to form a shape using pressure. The punch press may receive its computer program from an independently written CNC program or from a drafting program called CAD/CAM (Computer-Aided Drafting/Computer-Aided Manufacturing) program.

The CAD/CAM program will convert a drafted or modeled air conditioner part on the computer into a file that can be read by the punch press. The program tells the punch press where to punch holes in the sheet metal. The dies and other cutting instruments are stored in the punch press and can be mechanically brought to the punching arm for use in cutting the desired shape. The computer-controlled press brakes bend the sheet metal into its final form. Different bending dies are used to make different shapes.

3 Some support brackets that are made from sheet metal are produced on a hydraulic press or a mechanical press. A coiled sheet metal is unrolled as it is fed into the press, producing different shapes. High volumes of brackets can be made because the press can often produce a complex shape with one hit.

Some brackets, fins, and other air conditioner parts are manufactured by outside companies. They are brought into the assembly factory as needed. (Fins are thin aluminum strips that are bonded to the outer surface of evaporator and condenser coils. They help in the transfer of heat to and from the coils.)

Cleaning the parts

4 Different cleaning methods are used to remove dirt, oil, grease, and lubricants from the cut shapes that will make up the air conditioner. The parts may be soaked in large tanks filled with a cleaning solvent, which is stirred to remove the oil. Spray-wash systems using pressurized cleaning solutions may be used to knock off dirt and grease. Vapor degreasing may also be used. It involves hanging the parts above a harsh cleansing vapor, usually made of acid. As the vapor condenses (changes to liquid) on the metal surface, the grease and lubricants are removed.

Air conditioner parts that are manufactured by outside companies arrive at the assembly factory already degreased and cleaned. For additional corrosion protection, the parts may be put in a phosphate primer bath.

Powder coating

5 Before casings, pans, and brackets are assembled, they undergo a powder-coating process. First, the metal parts are charged with static electricity so the powder will stick to the bends and small openings within each part. As the parts are fed through a booth on an overhead conveyor belt, robotic sprayers cover the parts with a paint-like coating. Using the same conveyor system, the powder-coated parts are passed through an oven where the powder is permanently baked on the metal.

Bending the tubing for the condenser and evaporator

6 The condenser and evaporator are made of copper or aluminum tubing. Tubing arrives at the manufacturing factory in a large coil form. Before it can be processed in a bender to make the individual condenser and evaporator coils, the tubing goes through an uncoiler and straightener. Some straightened tubings are cut into desired lengths with an abrasive saw.

7 The tubing is formed into U-shaped bends with an computer-controlled bender, using the same principle as the press brake (see Step 2). A mandrel (a supporting bar) is inserted through the tubing, which is bent around a fixed mold. When the desired bend is achieved, the mandrel that kept the tube from collapsing during the bending process is pulled out. The finished evaporator and condenser coils are transported to the assembly area, where they are stacked on guide rods.

Aluminum plates are punched out using a punch press and formed on a mechanical press to place waves on the plates. These waves help in the transfer of heat.

Finishing the evaporator and condenser coils

8 Joining the evaporator coil with the aluminum plate constitutes a major part of the air conditioner assembly. The coil is mechanically fused to the aluminum plate by first inserting a mandrel through the tubing to expand it. Then the tubing is pushed against the inside part of the hole of the plate.

9 The condenser, on the other hand, is simply attached to a flat metal surface and is held in place by brackets. The condenser is connected to the evaporator with connecting devices, such as fittings and couplings.

Evaporator and condenser coils may be covered with aluminum fins. The fins are very fine precoated strips that are mounted all around the surface of the coils and are designed to transfer heat efficiently.

10 The expansion valve, also called a capillary tube, comes as a complete component. It is purchased from a vendor, and is installed in the piping after the condenser is in place.

Installing the pump

11 The pump, or compressor, is also purchased from a vendor. It is connected to the air conditioning system using fittings and couplings, and anchored in place by support brackets. It is bolted together with the other structural members of the system and is housed in the sheet metal casing. The casing is fastened to the base to protect the inner components.

Quality Control

Each component of the air conditioning system is checked at various stages of production. The different groups of workers responsible for specific stages of production typically have quality control plans to ascertain that the components they are working on are properly constructed. Once assembly of the air conditioner is complete, a performance test is done to ensure the whole system operates efficiently. Components purchased from outside vendors undergo inspection by quality assurance personnel before they are incorporated into the final product.

The Future

The Air Conditioning and Refrigeration Institute reports that almost half of all American homes have air conditioning. Industry experts predict that the market for air conditioners will continue to grow because manufacturers are quick to respond to consumers' changing needs.

Manufacturers continue to face the challenge of improving energy efficiency and lowering costs. Some manufacturers are producing systems with the highest SEER efficiency rating of 18 (see sidebar). High-powered compressors and alternate refrigerants that will eventually replace hydrochlorofluorocarbons (HCFCs) are being developed.

In the area of designs, new room models include compacts that do not take up much window space, technology that prevents water condensation, lightweight remote control, and soft-touch control pad. Outdoors units for central air conditioning come with a condenser coil that has specially coated aluminum fins and zinc-clad housing to prevent corrosion.

The competitiveness of the industry is not limited to just developing new designs and cost-effective systems. In 2001, Carrier Corporation took this competition to another level. The company has teamed up with IBM (International Business Machines Corporation) to introduce the first Web-enabled air conditioner that can communicate with personal computers and mobile telephones. Some of the features include consumer capability, when they are away from home, of turning their unit on and off and setting temperatures using the Internet. Repair persons will also be able to access air conditioner data and anticipate problems in the unit.

For More Information

Books

Althouse, Andrew D., Carl H. Turnquist, and Alfred F. Bracciano. *Modern Refrigeration and Air Conditioning*. Tinley Park, IL: The Goodheart-Willcox Company, Inc., 1996.

Killinger, Jerry, and LaDonna Killinger. *Heating and Cooling Essentials*. Tinley Park, IL: The Goodheart-Willcox Company, Inc., 1999.

Periodicals

"IBM and Carrier Team to Launch First Web-Enabled Air Conditioner." *Appliance* (May 2001): pp.15–16.

Ivins, Molly. "King of Cool." *Time*. (December 7, 1998): p. 109.

Web Sites

"Energy-Efficient Air Conditioning." *U.S. Department of Energy*. http://www.eren.doe.gov/erec/factsheets/aircond.html (accessed on July 22, 2002).

"Stay Cool! Air Conditioning America." *National Building Museum*. http://www.nbm.org/Exhibits/past/2000_1996/Stay_Cool!.html (accessed on July 22, 2002).

Animation

A nimation is a series of still (nonmoving) drawings that, when viewed one after the other at a fast pace, gives the impression of a moving picture. The word animation comes from the Latin *anima*, meaning breath or soul, and *animare*, meaning to fill with breath.

Since early history, people have used various ways of giving the impression of moving pictures. Drawings found in caves showed animals with legs overlapping so that they appeared to be running. Other art forms that exhibited some kind of animation include Asian puppet shows, Greek sculpture, Egyptian funeral paintings, medieval stained glass, and modern comic strips.

Walt Disney's first full-length animated movie, Snow White and the Seven Dwarfs (1937), consisted of approximately 477,000 photographed drawings.

Early experimenters

In 1640, a German Jesuit priest named Athanasius Kircher (1601–1680) invented a "magic lantern" that projected enlarged drawings on a wall. This invention is often considered the first movie projector. It consisted of a little tin box lit by candles and oil lamps and with a chimney on top. The "magic lantern" earned its name from its slide-show type of presentations of devils, ghosts, and goblins. Gaspar Schott (1608–1666), using his associate Kircher's idea, created a strip of pictures that was pulled across the lantern's lens (a piece of clear glass). He later changed the design of the lantern to a spinning disk (thin, flat, round plate).

Optical illusion

The popularity of magic-lantern shows grew with the discovery of the physical occurrence called "persistence of vision," by which the retina of the eye holds on to a still image for a fraction of a second longer after the eye has seen it. When a person views drawings of the different stages of an action, the eye sees one drawing blending into the next, so that the person has the mental impression of a continuous movement.

In 1832, Belgian scientist Joseph Plateau (1801–1883) invented the phenakistoscope, a cardboard spinning disk with holes. Pictures were drawn around the edges of the disk showing successive (arranged in order) movements. The viewer held the disk at eye level in front of a mirror and spun the disk, using a stick attached to its back. The reflection (the bouncing back) of the pictures passed through the holes, giving the illusion of movement. In Austria, Simon Ritter von Stampfer (1792–1864) made a similar device, calling it a stroboscope. In 1834, William George Horner (1786–1837) invented the zoetrope, in which a strip of pictures on the inside of a rotating drum were seen as moving objects through small openings in the outside of the drum.

Projecting pictures

In 1845, Baron Franz von Uchatius (1811–1881) of Austria invented the first movie projector, a device by which images painted on glass were passed in front of the projected light. In 1888, George Eastman (1854–1932) introduced celluloid film, a strip of celluloid acetate with a light-sensitive coating that retained and projected images better than glass.

Animated cartoons

In the United States, James Stuart Blackton (1875–1941) showed the first animated cartoon, *Humorous Phases of Funny Faces*, in 1906. As the Sunday comic strips gained popularity, other cartoonists, including Bud Fisher (1905–1954), who created *Mutt and Jeff*, and George Herriman (1880–1944), who created *Krazy Kat*, started doing animated films. However, among the early animators, Winsor McCay (1867–1934) stood out. McCay's animated film of his comic strip *Gertie the Dinosaur* (1914) is credited for raising the art of animation to a higher level with its lifelike character and the fluid movement of the film.

Felix the Cat was the most popular animated cartoon character before the introduction of sound. Created by Otto Messmer (1892–1983) in 1919, Felix easily became a model for drawing cartoon characters.

comic strip: A narrative series of cartoons.

dubbing: A rerecording from the original sound track.

frame: A single still (nonmoving) drawing, twenty-four of which are needed to make one second of animation.

magnetic tape: A thin ribbon of plastic coated with iron oxide and used to record sounds, images, or data.

persistence of vision: A physical phenomenon in which the retina of the eye holds on to an image for a fraction of a second longer after it has seen the image. The brain, which works with the eye, puts these still images together so that the eye perceives them as a single movement.

The 1914 film *Gertie the Dinosaur* is considered by many to be the first fully animated cartoon. *Reproduced by permission of The Kobal Collection.*

Walt Disney

In 1928, Walt Disney (1901–1966), with his associate Ub Iwerks, created the character Mickey Mouse. In 1928, the pair introduced their third Mickey Mouse film (the first two were soundless), *Steamboat Willie*, complete with voices and music. *Steamboat Willie* was an instant hit. Disney used color for the first time in 1932 in *Flowers and Trees*. His first full-length animated movie, *Snow White and the Seven Dwarfs*, came out in 1937. The movie consisted of approximately 477,000 photographed drawings. Translated into thirteen foreign languages, it went on to become the box-office favorite all over the world the following year. Other Disney favorites include *Dumbo* (1940), *Fantasia* (1940), and *Cinderella* (1950).

Moving on

Since the 1950s, filmmakers have experimented with new methods of animation, including pixilation, in which live people are filmed in different fixed poses to give the impression of humanly impossible movements.

rotoscope animation: A type of animation in which live actions are filmed first, images are traced and colored to create a series of animation cels, and then refilmed frame by frame.

sound track: The recorded dialogue, music, and sound effects in an animation production.

Storyboards, such as these created for the film *Shrek*, are often used to show how different scenes, characters, and settings will look in an animated film. *Reproduced by permission of AP/Wide World Photos.*

This method was used in 1968 in *Yellow Submarine* starring the Beatles. In 1978, *The Lord of the Rings*, directed by Ralph Bakshi (1938–) used rotoscope animation, in which live actions were filmed first. The images were then projected frame by frame onto a drawing surface. These images were traced and colored to create a series of animation cels and filmed again frame by frame.

By the late 1900s, animators were experimenting with computer technology to create animation. Movies such as the *Alien* and the *Star Wars* series used computer special effects to enhance their stories. In 1995, John Lassiter directed the Walt Disney film *Toy Story*, the first feature film created entirely with computer animation.

synchronizer: A device that makes the sound and actions occur at the same time.

Raw Materials

The most important raw material in creating an animated film is the imagination of the animator. However, a variety of supplies are needed to

From storyboard to movie screen: The lovable green ogre Shrek helped make the movie *Shrek* one of the top grossing animation films of all time, earning over $200 million worldwide. *Reproduced by permission of The Kobal Collection.*

help translate that creativity to material form. Some of the supplies are constructed by the animator; others are purchased.

The animator works at an animation stand, which has a baseboard. Register pegs hold the drawings on the baseboard. The animation stand also holds a camera, a work surface, and a platen (a clear sheet of glass or Plexiglas® plastic that holds the drawings in place).

The images are drawn on cels (short for celluloids, a type of plastic), drawing papers, or films. Most professional animation is drawn on cels, which are transparent (see-through) sheets five millimeters thick. Each cel measures about 10 inches by 12 inches (25.4 centimeters by 30.5 centimeters). The top edge of the cel, paper, or film is punched with holes to fit the register pegs on the animation stand and baseboard. The pegs keep the drawing surface taut.

Opaque inks and paints, as well as transparent dyes, are commonly used to draw the story. Felt-tip markers, crayons, and litho pencils can also be used.

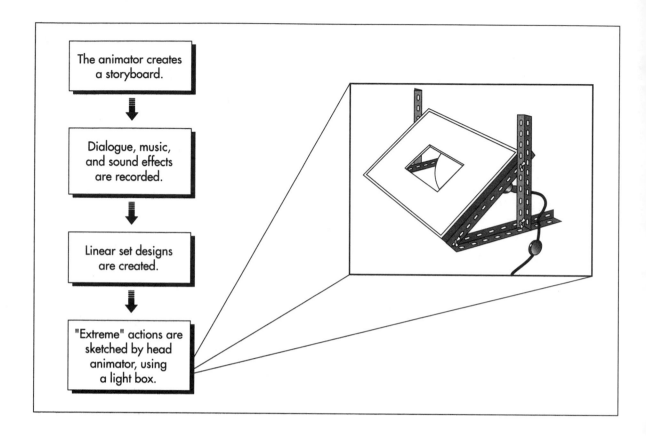

The animator creates a storyboard.

↓

Dialogue, music, and sound effects are recorded.

↓

Linear set designs are created.

↓

"Extreme" actions are sketched by head animator, using a light box.

The animation is photographed using 35-millimeter cameras. Some animators use Super 8 or 16-millimeter models. Different camera lenses are used, including standard, zoom, telephoto, wide-angle, and fish-eye lenses.

The Manufacturing Process

The creation of an animated film, whether short or full-length, is a time-consuming process. The average short film requires about 45,000 separate frames. A frame is a still (nonmoving) drawing A total of twenty-four frames per minute are needed to give the illusion of movement.

The story is written

1 The animator may also be the writer of the story. The writer makes a storyboard, which is a series of one-panel sketches pinned on a base-board. It looks just like a big comic strip. Dialogue and/or sum-maries of action are written under each sketch. The sketches may be

rearranged several times depending on how the writer, the animator, and the director wish to present the story.

The dialogue, music, and sound effects are recorded

2 Actors record the voices of each character. Background music and sound effects, such as footsteps, the opening and closing of doors, and popcorn popping, are recorded on magnetic tapes.

The music is timed for beats and accents. This music information is recorded on a bar sheet so that the animation can be fitted around the music. This process of fitting the actions to the music is called "Mickey Mousing," named after the popular character whose creator, Walt Disney, was one of the first do so.

Many animation studios now use an optical sound track on which voices, music, and sound effects are represented by varying lines. An electronic sound reader and synchronizer give an accurate count of the number of frames needed for each sound.

Dialogue measurements are entered on an exposure sheet

3 A technician called a track reader measures each vowel and consonant in the dialogue. Words are recorded on exposure sheets (also called x-sheets or dope sheets). Each sheet represents a single film frame. This allows the animators to synchronize (let occur at the same time) each movement of the character's lips with the dialogue.

Footage, the time needed between lines of dialogue for the action to occur, is also recorded on the exposure sheet. Slugs, sections of film without sound, are inserted where the action occurs.

Model character sheets are created

4 A model of each character is made to ensure his or her appearance is the same throughout the film. The models can be detailed descriptions. They can also be sketches of the characters in different positions with various facial expressions.

Artists create the layout or set design

5 A layout artist creates linear drawings that animators use as a guide for action. Background artists use these same drawings for painting the backgrounds.

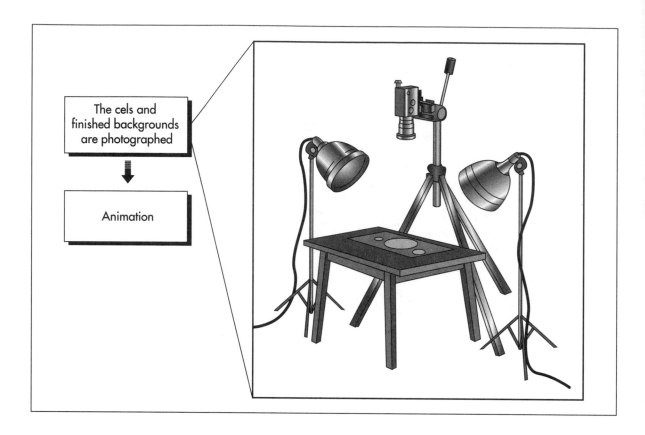

The cels and
finished backgrounds
are photographed

↓

Animation

Characters' actions are sketched

6 The head animator uses the model character sheets to sketch the primary actions. For example, if the character is running, the head animator will draw three to five or six frames out of the twenty-four needed per second to create animation. One drawing will be of a foot leaving the floor, the next of the foot in the air, and a third of a foot returning to the floor. The details in between these three "extreme" actions will then be filled in by the animation assistants, sometimes called the "in-betweeners."

The drawing is done on a transparent drawing board that is lighted from below. After a drawing sheet is done, a second sheet is placed on top of the first. The second sheet is drawn slightly different from the first to show movement.

Drawings are cleaned up and checked for accuracy

7 Artists compare characters drawn against the model sheets. Drawings may be made sharper but not changed. Scenes are checked to ensure they include all actions recorded on the exposure sheet. The

artists also make sure the characters are properly lined up with the background.

A video test is conducted

8 The animators make a computerized video-tape of the sketches to check for smoothness of movements and proper facial expressions. Adjustments are made as needed.

Artists create background

9 The artists create color backgrounds, including landscapes, scenery, buildings, and interiors. These are done using the linear drawings. The artists then use a computer to fill in the color. As the computer scans (reads) the layout, the artists click on colors from a template, or a palette of colors.

Sketches are inked in and painted

10 If the animation drawings have been done on paper, they are transferred to cels using a photocopying process. In some studios, a person known as an inker traces the pencil sketches onto the cels, using a special ink that sticks to the cels. Colors are applied to the other side of the cels, using the same computer process to color the background. All inked and colored materials are checked for accuracy.

The action is filmed

11 The cels and backgrounds are photographed following the instructions on the exposure sheet. One scene of actions can take several hours to photograph. The cels are placed on top of the backgrounds and photographed from above. As more characters appear in a frame, more cels are stacked on the background. Each level of cels is lighted up and staggered to make the resulting pictures seem three-dimensional (having height, weight, and depth). Then, the film is sent to the photo lab, where a print and a negative are made.

The sound is dubbed

12 Dialogue, music, and sound effects are rerecorded from several tracks into one sound track. Two other sound tracks—the dialogue and music—are made. These will be used for translation when the film is sent to foreign countries.

CELS

A very important development in animation was the introduction of clear sheets of celluloids (cels) on which drawings were made. Patented in 1914 by American Earl Hurd (1880–1940), cels allowed the placing of different drawings of movements on top of a single background scene. This way the artist did not have to draw the same background over and over, allowing more time to add details to the fewer background scenes needed, as well as to the characters.

The dubbing track and print are combined

13 The final dubbed track is combined with the print to make one unit called a "married print." If the animated film is for television viewing, the negative and the married print are usually sent to a video postproduction house to be converted to videotape.

The Future

Computer-generated animation continues its popularity. In the summer of 2001, *Shrek,* one of the most popular animated movies of all time, was produced with the aid of more than 1,000 computers. Anime, a cartoon form that started in Japan after World War II (1939–45), has become popular worldwide. The characters and movements are more detailed and realistic. Varied camera angles give viewers a clearer look at the actions.

For More Information

Books

Charnan, Simon. *Walt Disney: Creator of Magical Worlds.* New York, NY: Children's Press, 1999.

Hahn, Don. *Animation Magic: A Behind-the-Scenes Look at How an Animated Film Is Made.* New York, NY: Disney Press, 1996.

O'Donnell, Annie. *Computer Animator.* New York, NY: The Rosen Publishing Group, Inc., 2000.

Periodicals

Ansen, David. "The *Shrek* Effect: This jolly green giant is putting the squeeze on Disney's Mouse House, raising the bar on animation and threatening to steal the first Oscar in the field." *Newsweek.* (June 18, 2001): pp. 50-51.

Web Sites

Burns, Paul T. "The Complete History of the Discovery of Cinematography." http://www.precinemahistory.net (accessed on July 22, 2002).

"How We Make A Movie: Pixar's Animation Process." *Pixar Animation Studios.* http://www.pixar.com/howwedoit/index.html (accessed July 22, 2002).

Antibiotic

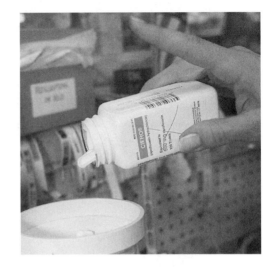

A n antibiotic is a chemical substance made by a living microorganism (a living thing that is so small it can only be seen through a microscope), such as a fungus or mold, that is harmful to another microorganism that causes diseases. An antibiotic drug can stop the growth of harmful bacteria and other microorganisms, or destroy them. More than ten thousand antibiotic substances have been found. Scientists can also make antibiotics synthetically (artificially) from chemicals or from a combination of chemicals and natural substances (semisynthetic drugs). The production of antibiotics has become a multibillion-dollar industry that continues to grow each year.

The production of antibiotics has become a multibillion-dollar industry that continues to grow each year.

Over 2,500 years old

Although the process by which antibiotics fight disease-causing bacteria was not discovered until the twentieth century, the Chinese had used antibiotics about 2,500 years ago. They discovered that applying the moldy curd of soybeans to the body could heal certain infections (conditions resulting from the body's invasion by disease-causing microorganisms).

Other cultures are also known to have used antibiotic-type substances to cure illnesses. The Sudanese-Nubian civilization used a type of tetracycline antibiotic as early as 350 C.E. (common era). In Europe during the Middle Ages (476–1453), crude plant extracts and cheese curds were used to fight infections.

Modern antibiotics

agar: A gelatin-like substance in which scientists grow organisms.

bacteria: Small, one-celled organisms that can only be seen through a microscope.

culture: A growth of microorganisms in nutrient.

infection: Invasion of the body by disease-causing microorganisms.

ion-exchange method: A method of purifying a water-soluble antibiotic that is collected after fermentation. The antibiotic is first separated from the waste materials in the fermentation broth, then sent through equipment that separates other water-soluble materials from the antibiotic.

microorganism: A living thing that is so small it can only be seen through a microscope.

Modern antibiotics resulted from the work of several individuals who demonstrated that materials derived from certain microorganisms could be used to cure infectious diseases. In 1877, French chemist and microbiologist Louis Pasteur (1822–1895) discovered that disease-causing anthrax bacteria could be prevented from multiplying by *Saprophyte* bacteria living on dead and decaying organisms. Anthrax, a disease that dates back to biblical times, can be fatal, sometimes affecting a large number of animals. The disease also affects humans.

The first miracle drug

In 1928, Scottish bacteriologist Alexander Fleming (1881–1955) made one of the most important contributions to the field of antibiotics. While culturing (growing) *Staphyloccus* bacteria in a laboratory dish, Fleming made a remarkable discovery. He found that mold, which had grown on some bacteria, prevented their growth. Upon further investigation, Fleming found that a substance in the mold *Penicillium notatum* could destroy many disease-producing bacteria without harming healthy body cells.

However, Fleming was unable to develop penicillin for medical use. It was not until 1941 that Ernst Chain (1906–1979) and Howard Florey (1898–1968), continuing Fleming's work, developed the drug penicillin. Penicillin was later called the "miracle drug" because of its role in saving millions of human lives. Penicillin remains one of the effective treatments for such bacterial infections as pneumonia, strep throat, and syphilis.

Other antibiotics

Since the development of penicillin, other antibiotic substances have been found. In 1939, research began on identifying possible antibiotic materials from the soil bacteria *Streptomyces*. In 1943, Ukrainian-born American microbiologist Selman Waksman (1888–1973) developed the drug streptomycin from soil bacteria. It was the first antibiotic found effective in treating tuberculosis.

In 1941, Waksman coined the term antibiotic—from the Greek *anti*, meaning against, and *bios*, meaning life. The term describes the drug's function of fighting bacteria either by killing them or by preventing them from multiplying.

After World War II (1939–1945), the search for molds and other soil bacteria led to the development of other antibiotics, including erythromycin and cephalosporin that can each be used in patients allergic to penicillin. Quinolone, which was developed during the 1960s, has been used in treating urinary-tract infections and infectious diarrhea. Since the 1970s, most antibiotics produced have been the synthetic types.

How antibiotics work

Antibiotics fight harmful bacteria in different ways. Some antibiotics destroy bacteria by weakening their cell walls, causing the walls to burst. Certain antibiotics damage the exterior of bacterial cells, causing the contents of the cells to leak. Still other antibiotics interfere with the bacteria's metabolism, the chemical processes in the cells needed by the bacteria to multiply and function. For example, tetracycline interferes with the production of proteins, which not only make up structural parts of the bacteria but also perform important functions.

Sir Alexander Fleming co-discovered penicillin, an antibiotic that helped cure people of many once-fatal bacterial infections. *Reproduced by permission of Corbis Corporation.*

Raw Materials

Antibiotics are produced using a fermentation process. The substances that make up the fermentation broth are the raw materials needed to manufacture antibiotics. This broth contains all the ingredients needed to promote the growth of the specific antibiotic-producing microorganisms.

The fermentation broth typically contains a carbon source, such as molasses or soy meal, which are made up of lactose and glucose. These are the food sources for the microorganisms. Ammonia is added for its nitrogen, which the organisms need for metabolism. Trace elements are added for proper growth. They include phosphorus, sulfur, magnesium, zinc, iron, and copper. Anti-foaming substances are added to prevent foaming.

nutrient: A food substance, such as carbohydrate, protein, fat, mineral, vitamin, water, or fiber needed for growth.

organism: Any living thing.

pH: A number that shows the acidity or alkalinity of a chemical substance.

semisynthetic antibiotic: An antibiotic that is made from a combination of chemicals and natural substances.

solvent-extraction: A method of purifying an oil-soluble antibiotic that is collected after fermentation. The fermentation broth is treated with substances that can dissolve the antibiotic, and the antibiotic is collected using chemical means.

starter culture: A small growth of microorganisms used to start a larger growth to produce antibiotics.

synthetic antibiotic: An antibiotic that is made artificially from chemicals.

Phamacists help keep track of all the antibiotics a patient is taking and also answer any questions there might be about different medications. *Reproduced by permission of Custom Medical Stock Photo, Inc.*

The Manufacturing Process

Although most antibiotics are found in nature, they do not normally occur in the amounts necessary to produce a great quantity. For this reason, a fermentation process has been developed. It involves collecting the microorganism whose antibiotic product is desired, promoting the increase in numbers of the culture (growth of the specific microorganism in a laboratory), and separating the excreted antibiotic product from the fermentation broth.

CONSUMERS LACK KNOWLEDGE OF ANTIBIOTIC USE

The misuse and overuse of antibiotics have encouraged the spread of bacterial resistance to antibiotics. Patients sometimes ask their doctors to prescribe antibiotics for the common cold and flu (influenza), which are caused by viruses and cannot be cured by antibiotics. Some doctors tend to prescribe antibiotics for all kinds of symptoms. For an antibiotic to work, the patient has to take the complete prescription. It is very common for patients to stop taking the prescription once the symptoms of the illness have disappeared. Some people do not know that even if they feel better after several days of medication, some of the bacteria that cause the infection live on and continue to multiply. Stopping the medication makes the surviving bacteria resistant to the drug. If the person develops the same illness in the future and is prescribed the same antibiotic, it may not work.

A 1998 survey of the American public by the American Society of Health-System Pharmacists, Bethesda, Maryland, found that:

Over one-third of Americans surveyed said they stopped taking their complete antibiotic prescription because they started feeling better.

About 1 out of 4 people said they saved antibiotics prescribed for one illness and then took them for another illness at a later time.

More than half thought antibiotics are the best medicine for viral infections.

Starting the culture

1 Before fermentation can begin, the desired antibiotic-producing organism is collected and made to multiply. This is done by producing an initial, or sample, culture. This initial culture is cultivated in a dish with agar (a gelatin-like substance that acts as an environment in which organisms grow). Then, the initial culture is transferred into shake flasks (bottle-like containers) with growth-promoting nutrients added. The starter culture is allowed to multiply some more.

2 The starter culture is transferred to seed tanks for further growth. The seed tanks are steel tanks filled with all the food and nutrients the specific microorganisms need to survive and grow. These include warm water, carbohydrate foods, such as lactose or glucose sugars, and nutrients like those found in the shake flasks. The tanks also contain carbon sources, such as acetic acid, alcohols, or hydrocarbons, as well as nitrogen sources, such as ammonia salts. Air that is sterilized (germ-free) and filtered (rid of impurities) is delivered into the tank, while mixers keep the mixture moving. After about twenty-four to twenty-eight hours, the mixture is transferred to fermentation tanks.

virus: A very tiny particle than can grow inside a living cell. Viruses attack the cells of other organisms to make copies of themselves. Outside a cell, viruses are lifeless. Viruses cause such illnesses as the flu, colds, and AIDS.

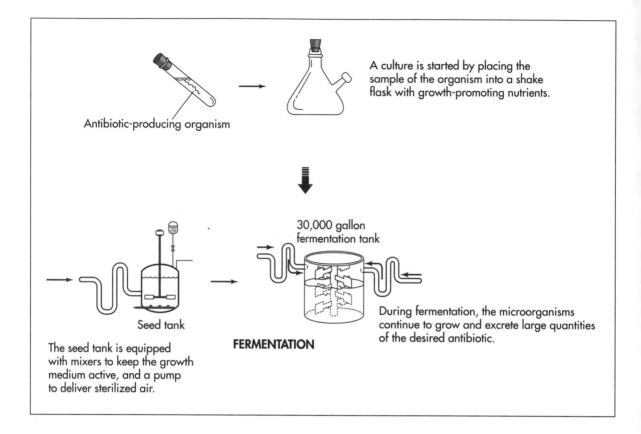

Antibiotic-producing organism

A culture is started by placing the sample of the organism into a shake flask with growth-promoting nutrients.

30,000 gallon fermentation tank

Seed tank

During fermentation, the microorganisms continue to grow and excrete large quantities of the desired antibiotic.

The seed tank is equipped with mixers to keep the growth medium active, and a pump to deliver sterilized air.

FERMENTATION

Fermentation

3 The fermentation tank is a bigger version of the seed tank and holds about 30,000 gallons. It is filled with the same ingredients found in the seed tank to encourage further growth of the microorganisms. The tank temperature is kept between 73 to 81 degrees Fahrenheit (23 to 27.2 degrees Centigrade). The mixture is constantly stirred, and sterilized, and filtered air is continuously pumped in. For this reason, antifoaming agents are periodically added. Acids or bases are added as needed to keep a pH balance that is ideal for growth. In this environment, the microorganisms continue to grow and multiply and excrete large quantities of the desired antibiotic.

Isolation and purification

4 After three to five days, when the maximum amount of antibiotic has been produced, the process of collecting the antibiotic from the broth starts. Different purification methods are used, depending on the type of antibiotic produced.

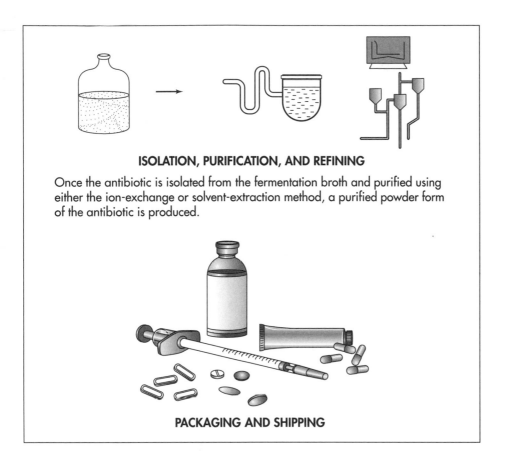

ISOLATION, PURIFICATION, AND REFINING

Once the antibiotic is isolated from the fermentation broth and purified using either the ion-exchange or solvent-extraction method, a purified powder form of the antibiotic is produced.

PACKAGING AND SHIPPING

5 For antibiotics that are water-soluble (can be dissolved in water), an ion-exchange method is used. The antibiotic is separated from the waste materials in the fermentation broth. Then, it is separated from other water-soluble materials. For antibiotics that are oil-soluble (can be dissolved in oil), a solvent-extraction method is used. The fermentation broth is treated with butyl acetate or methyl isobutyl ketone, substances that can dissolve the antibiotic. The antibiotic is then collected using chemical means. These methods produce a purified powdered form of the antibiotic, which is further converted into different product forms.

Refining

6 Antibiotics can come in different forms. They can come in solutions for intravenous (given by injection) bags or syringes (needles) and in pill or gel-capsule form. They can be in the form of powders that are added to topical ointments (creams applied to a body part).

Based on the final form of the antibiotic, different refining steps are used. For intravenous bags, the crystalline antibiotic is dissolved in a solution and put in the bag, which is then hermetically sealed (tightly sealed so that air cannot get in). For gel capsules, powdered antibiotic is put into the capsule bottom; the top half of the capsule is then put in place. For topical ointments, the antibiotic is mixed into the ointment.

7 Finally, the antibiotic products are transported to the packaging stations. The products are stacked and put in boxes. They are loaded up on trucks and transported to hospitals, pharmacies, and various distributors.

Quality Control

A germ-free environment has to be maintained throughout the manufacturing process, so that other microorganisms do not contaminate (introduce impurities to) the culture. The culture medium and all the processing equipment are steam-sterilized. Moreover, frequent checks of the condition of the culture during fermentation are conducted. The finished product is further checked for its physical and chemical properties, including pH, melting point, and moisture content.

In the United States, the Food and Drug Administration (FDA) regulates the production of antibiotics. The amount of testing depends on the type of antibiotic and how it will be used. For example, the FDA might require that, for a particular antibiotic, it has to first check each batch for effectiveness and purity before giving its approval for sale to the public.

The Future

Since the earliest use of antibiotics against disease-causing bacteria, some of these harmful microorganisms have developed drug resistance so that they cannot be killed or controlled by the antibiotic. Typically, an antibiotic destroys most bacteria that are making a person ill; however, a few bacteria may manage to survive. These bacteria develop resistance genes (basic units of hereditary materials) that are passed down to their offspring or transferred to others within the same species (a group of living things that have similar characteristics). Gene exchange is a common occurrence among organisms. Experts have found that resistant bacteria tend to fight off more than one antibiotic.

A renewed interest

According to the U.S. Centers for Disease Control and Prevention (CDC), cases of antibiotic resistance are increasing. Life-threatening diseases, such as tuberculosis, are on the rise. Realizing the threat to public health, drug companies all over the world are taking up the challenge of developing new antibiotics to fight microorganisms that are resistant to antibiotics.

One area of interest is sparked by the Human Genome Project, an international research program designed to understand the genomes of humans and organisms. (The genome is the complete collection of genes passed down from generation to generation.) For example, some scientists have been able to map out the genome of the bacterium that infects the lungs of cystic fibrosis patients. This antibiotic-resistant bacterium destroys the patient's lungs, eventually causing death. By studying the genome, scientists hope to develop an antibiotic that would target some part of the bacterium, thus destroying it. Researchers continue to look for newer types of antibiotics, as well as a combination of drugs to fight resistant bacteria. Scientists are also trying to develop vaccines to prevent bacterial infections.

For More Information

Books

Gottfried, Ted. *Alexander Fleming: Discoverer of Penicillin.* New York, NY: Franklin Watts, 1997.

Levy, Stuart B. *The Antibiotic Paradox: How the Misuse of Antibiotics Endangers Their Curative Power.* Cambridge, MA: Perseus Publishing, 2001.

Periodicals

Bren, Linda. "Antibiotic Resistance From Down on the Chicken Farm." *FDA Consumer.* (January-February 2001): pp. 10-11

Monroe, Judy. "Antibiotics vs. the Superbugs." *Current Health 2.* (October 2001): pp. 24-25.

Web Sites

"An Inside Look at FDA On-Site." *Center for Drug Evaluation and Research, Food and Drug Administration.* http://www.fda.gov/cder/about/whatwedo/testtube-7.pdf (accessed on July 22, 2002).

Artificial Heart

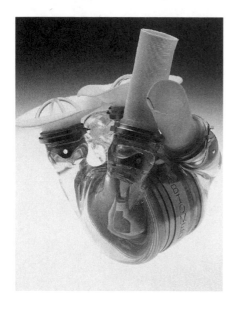

AbioCor™ artificial heart. *Reproduced by permission of AP/Wide World Photos.*

According to the American Heart Association, an estimated 550,000 new cases of heart failure are diagnosed each year.

An artificial heart is a device designed to completely replace a seriously damaged heart, temporarily take over the function of a failing heart until a donor heart is available for heart transplant, or perform the job of a natural heart during surgery. The two major types of artificial heart are the heart-lung machine and the mechanical heart. The heart-lung machine consists of a pump, which performs the heart's job of pumping blood, and an oxygenator, which performs the lungs' job of supplying oxygen to the blood. This machine is mainly used by surgeons to stop and restart the heart during heart surgery.

A mechanical heart, on the other hand, may be a self-contained artificial heart or a left ventricular assist device (LVAD). The self-contained artificial heart is designed for patients who cannot be helped by any other means and are not eligible for heart transplant. It is also called a total artificial heart because it contains its own power source. The LVAD, on the other hand, is designed to work alongside the heart, taking on the workload of the left ventricle while the patient awaits a heart transplant. The left ventricle, responsible for the pumping action of the heart, is the hardest working of the four chambers (sections) of the heart. It performs about 80 percent of the heart's work and, as such, is usually the part that is weakened by disease.

A tireless worker

The heart is a hard-working organ that continually moves blood throughout the whole body. It has four chambers. The upper chambers, or the atria (singular: atrium), receive the blood that flows back to the heart through the veins. The lower chambers, or the ventricles, pump the blood out of the heart through the arteries.

Blood enters the right atrium through the veins and fills the right atrium. The right atrium pumps the blood through a valve into the right ventricle, which in turn pumps the blood to the lungs through another valve. The person breathes out carbon dioxide and breathes in oxygen. The oxygen-rich blood goes back to the heart, entering through the left atrium. The left atrium sends the blood into the left ventricle, which pumps it out to the body through the aorta, the largest artery of the body. Smaller blood vessels branching out of the aorta carry the blood to different parts of the body.

Heart failure

Congestive heart failure is the steadily declining ability of the heart to pump blood. It is one of the leading causes of death. Some people are born with a defective heart or may have caught a virus that damaged the heart. In others, the disease may be caused by high blood pressure, sudden damage from a heart attack, or other medical problems. Still others have developed the disease as a result of smoking, eating foods high in fat and cholesterol, not exercising, or being overweight. According to the American Heart Association, almost five million Americans suffer from heart failure, and an estimated 550,000 new cases are diagnosed each year. Although it usually affects older people, heart failure is also seen in children and young people.

First artificial hearts

Since the late 1800s, medical researchers have tried to develop a mechanical device to temporarily take over the heart's function of pumping blood. In 1935, American surgeon John H. Gibbon (1903–73) invented

alloy: A mixture of a metal and a nonmetal or a mixture of two or more metals.

aorta: The main artery that carries blood away from the heart to the different parts of the body.

artery: A blood vessel that carries blood away from the heart.

the first heart-lung machine. It took him nearly twenty years to perfect his invention. In 1953, Gibbon used the machine to perform the first open-heart surgery on an 18-year-old patient. Four years later, Dr. Willem Kolff (1911–), a Dutch-born physician, implanted the first artificial heart into a dog.

While Kolff was working on building a total artificial heart, other researchers were developing artificial devices for patients who were waiting for a heart transplant or for those whose hearts were not functioning fully. In 1963, Dr. Michael DeBakey (1908–) implanted a pump with internal valves in a patient. The plastic banana-shaped device helped move the blood through the chambers of the heart. In 1966, Dr. Adrian Kantrowitz (1918–) implanted a partial mechanical heart in a human. That same year, DeBakey implanted the first LVAD.

Denton Cooley (1920–) and his surgical team at the Texas Heart Institute (Houston, Texas) performed the first temporary human artificial heart implant in 1969, using a device designed by Argentine-born Domingo Liotta (1924–). The artificial heart was a double-ventricle pump, made of plastic and synthetic polyester fabric. It was air-driven by an external console, a cabinet-like structure about the size of a home washing machine with a control panel. The artificial heart kept Haskell Karp alive for almost three days, after which time he had a heart transplant.

A complete replacement heart

The first time that an artificial heart totally replaced a diseased human heart occurred on December 2, 1982. Dr. William DeVries (1943–) implanted the *Jarvik-7* heart into Barney Clark (1921–1983). Clark was too sick to qualify for a donor heart, so the device would be a permanent heart for the 61-year-old patient. Named after its inventor, Dr. Robert Jarvik (1946–), the artificial heart was slightly bigger than the human heart and weighed about the same (10 ounces, or 280 grams). The device was made of plastic on an aluminum base and consisted of two pumping ventricles (lower heart chambers) connected to the upper chambers of the patient's heart. The pumping action came from compressed air delivered by an electrical console outside the patient's body. Two air hoses, inserted through abdominal incisions (cuts), were connected to the artificial ventricles. Clark survived for 112 days before finally dying from infection and blood vessel blockage resulting from blood clots.

DeVries performed four other implants using the *Jarvik-7*. The patients eventually died, including William Schroeder (1932–1986), who lived for 620 days. Further ventures in inventing a permanent artificial heart came

atrium: One of the two upper chambers of the heart that receives blood from the veins and pumps it to the ventricles.

blood clot: A solid mass of blood that can block the movement of blood.

chamber: One of the four sections of the heart through which blood is pumped.

donor heart: A healthy heart obtained from a person who has just died and used for such purposes as a heart transplant. Persons who have voluntarily given permission for their organs to be used after their death typically carry a donor card, stating their intent.

heart transplant: Also called heart transplantation; the process of replacing a diseased heart with a healthy heart from a person who has just died.

to a halt, especially because of the problems encountered in its use—the formation of blood clots that traveled to the brain, causing strokes; the occurrence of infection due to the abdominal incisions and the opening of the patient's chest during surgery; and the patient's inability to move around because of the bulky console that was about the size of a home refrigerator.

Redesigning the artificial heart

In the 1990s, medical researchers turned their attention to designing mechanical devices to help weakened hearts function until a donor heart was available. In 1994, the U.S. Food and Drug Administration (FDA), the government agency responsible for approving medical devices, approved such a device. The HeartMate® Implantable Pneumatic Left Ventricular Assist System (IP LVAS) was a titanium alloy pump

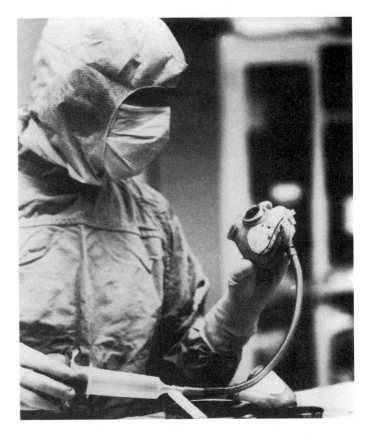

Dr. Robert Jarvik prepares the *Jarvik-7* mechanical heart for implantation. *Reproduced by permission of AP/Wide World Photos.*

implanted in the abdominal area and connected to the left ventricle. From the left ventricle, the device pumped the blood into the aorta, supplying the whole body with blood. The device was powered by an external console on a movable cart, which ran on electricity or battery (for thirty minutes).

In 1998, the FDA approved portable versions of the LVAD that are powered by a small external battery-run computerized controller worn at the waist or under the arm. The two rechargeable batteries have to be charged every six to eight hours. The devices usually have backup batteries and a hand pump that the patient can operate.

Design

Several important issues must be addressed when designing a LVAD. The designer has to make sure that enough blood is pumped. The exter-

stroke: A sudden blockage or bursting of a blood vessel in the brain, interrupting the blood flow to part of the brain.

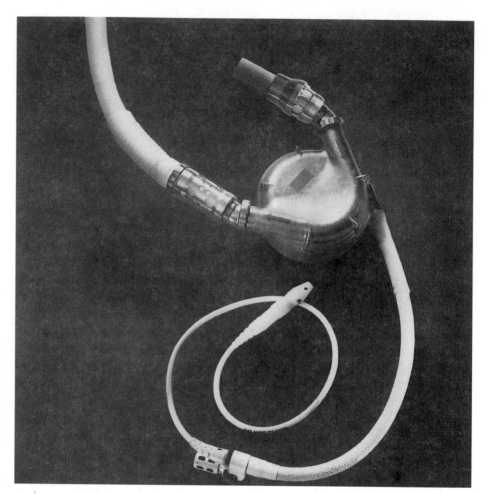

The HeartMate® XVE is the enhanced version of the HeartMate® VE, which is the world's most widely used implantable left ventricular assist device, or LVAD. *Reproduced courtesy of Thoratec Corporation.*

valve: In living hearts, one of the four flaps of tissue between the chambers that prevents the backward flow of blood. In artificial hearts, the flap-like structure that allows blood to flow in one direction.

vein: A blood vessel that returns blood to the heart.

ventricle: Either of the two lower chambers of the heart, which receives blood from the atria, or upper chambers, and pumps it into the arteries.

nal console must have a fixed mode as well as an automatic mode so that the pump can be adjusted to adapt to the patient's needs. The fixed mode ensures that the pump rate is the same all the time, while the automatic mode enables the system to make adjustments to the blood flow depending on what the patient requires.

The designer must also make sure that no blood clots are created. Materials must be biocompatible, which means that they must be able to coexist with the body tissue and not be rejected by it. Otherwise, the pump could fail. For the same reason, the total weight and size are important considerations. Some LVADs weigh as little as 1.25 pounds (570 grams) and measure about 2 inches (5 centimeters) thick and 4 inches (10 centimeters) in diameter. In addition, the motor must run at its most efficient level so that minimal heat is generated.

A LVAD pump generally consists of a blood chamber, an air chamber, inflow and outflow tubes, and a driveline for connecting to the external power source. The inflow tube attached to the left ventricle moves the blood to the blood chamber. An external control starts the pumping action. A pusher plate "pushes" the flexible diaphragm (separating membrane between the two chambers) upward, thus pressurizing the air chamber. This action ejects the blood through the outflow tube attached to the aorta, pumping the blood to all parts of the body.

Raw Materials

Since the left ventricle is the hardest-working of the four chambers of the heart, it is the most likely to get weak. The completely implantable artificial heart (the AbioCor™; see The Future) is still undergoing human testing; therefore, LVADs, currently the most widely used of the artificial hearts, will be discussed here. As of 2002, over 4,000 LVADs had been implanted in patients worldwide waiting for a heart transplant.

The LVAD is made of metal, plastic, ceramic, and animal parts. A titanium-aluminum-vanadium alloy is used for the pump and for other metal parts because it not rejected by the patient's body. The titanium parts are shaped at a specialized titanium processor and, except for surfaces that will have contact with blood, the titanium is given a certain finish. Blood-contacting surfaces are bonded with special titanium microspheres, which are tiny beads of titanium that produce textured surfaces.

A diaphragm within the pump is made from plastic polyurethane that is also textured. The textured surfaces of the titanium and the diaphragm are very important. When blood comes in contact with the textured surfaces, it deposits circulating blood cells, which stick to the surfaces, creating a living lining inside the device that resembles the inner surfaces of veins (blood vessels that return blood to the heart) and arteries (blood vessels that carry blood away from the heart). This helps prevent the formation of blood clots inside the LVAD.

The two tubular grafts that are used to attach the LVAD to the aorta and the left ventricle are made from polyester. The valves used are actual heart valves from a pig. The motor is made from titanium or other metals and ceramics.

The Manufacturing Process

Most components of the LVAD are made according to specifications by third-party manufacturers, including machine shops and manufacturers of the printed circuit board. A medical-device firm that specializes in heart valves sews the valves inside the tubular grafts with sutures.

Forming the plastic polyurethane parts

1 Some LVAD manufacturers make their own plastic polyurethane parts. One process uses a plastic liquid solution that is made by the manufacturer. This solution is poured on a ceramic mold layer by layer. Each layer is heated and dried until the desired thickness is achieved. The part is then removed from the mold and inspected. The polyurethane parts may be made by an outside manufacturer using injection molding, in which melted plastic is forced into a mold under high pressure and then allowed to cool. As it cools, the plastic assumes the shape of the mold.

Assembly

2 Each LVAD takes several days to assemble and test. The assembly takes place in a clean room to avoid contamination. Each LVAD consists of up to fifty components that are put together with special adhesives that have been strengthened at high temperatures.

3 Several assembly operations are done at the same time, including the assembly of the motor housing and components, the attachment of the pusher plate to the polyurethane diaphragm, and the assembly of the percutaneous tube. The percutaneous (administered through the skin) tube, as its name implies, is a small tube containing control and power wires that pass through the patient's skin and connect the LVAD to the power source. These subassemblies are individually inspected. The complete system is then put together. The tubular grafts are assembled separately and attached during surgery.

Testing

4 After the components are put together, each device is tested, using special equipment that mimics conditions the device would encounter once implanted in the body. All electronic parts are also tested to ensure the proper functioning of all electric circuitry.

Sterilization and packaging

5 After the LVAD has passed the testing, it is sent to an outside service for sterilization to destroy germs that may cause infection. Each device is sealed in plastic trays and returned to the heart manufacturer. It is then packaged in specially made suitcases to protect it from contamination and to prevent damage.

The Future

Heart disease remains the number one cause of death in the United States. As baby boomers (people born between 1946 and 1964) age, the number of people in need of healthy hearts will increase dramatically. Each year, an estimated 45,000 Americans need a heart transplant; however fewer than 3,000 donor hearts are available. Faced with this problem, scientists continue to develop artificial hearts as potential alternatives.

On July 2, 2001, the first-ever completely self-contained artificial heart (with power supply included) was implanted in a human. Drs. Laman Gray and Robert Dowling of the University of Louisville, Kentucky, removed Robert Tools's damaged heart, while leaving major blood vessels on which to attach the AbioCor™ Implantable Replacement Heart. Jointly developed by the Texas Heart Institute and Abiomed, Inc., the device is about the size of a softball and weighs 2 pounds (907

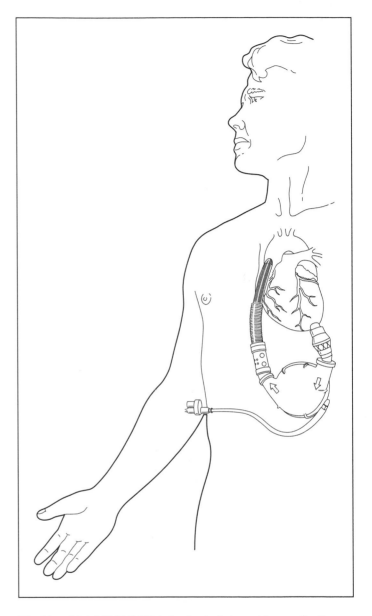

The HeartMate® XVE LVAD is implanted alongside a patient's own heart. The central blood pump is placed just below the diaphragm in the abdomen and is attached between the patient's heart and aorta. Wires attached to an external, wearable battery pack allow complete patient mobility.

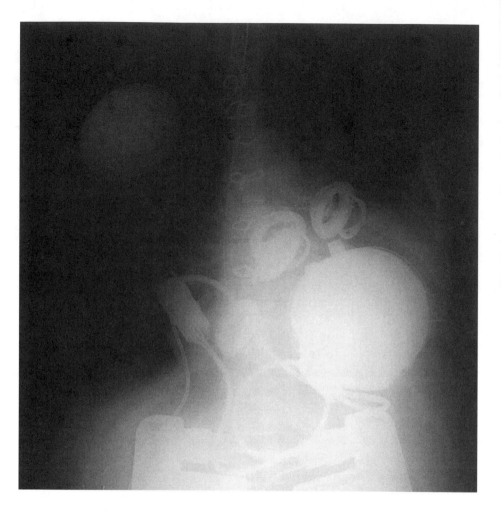

This X-ray shows the AbioCor™, an experimental heart, that was implanted in a man in July 2001. The device includes an internal rechargeable battery and a controller that regulates the pumping speed. *Reproduced by permission of AP/Wide World Photos.*

grams). Robert Tools died on November 30, 2001, from complications, which, according to his doctors, were unrelated to his artificial heart. Tom Christerson became the world's second recipient of the AbioCor™ Implantable Replacement Heart on September 13, 2001. Prior to his artificial-heart surgery, Christerson was not expected to live more than a month. On April 16, 2002, he was able to go home to his family. As of June 18, 2002, Drs. Gray and Dowling announced that the patient was doing well.

The AbioCor™ heart is powered by an external battery that passes electricity through the patient's skin (without any skin piercing) to a power receptor in the chest. An electronic monitor is implanted in the abdominal area to regulate the pumping speed. An internal battery continually charged by the external batteries serves as an emergency power source, as well as allows the patient to perform certain activities, such as take a shower, without the batteries. In January 2002, the manufacturer of AbioCor™ announced that it had removed a plastic cage in the design that may have caused blood clotting and led to stroke in at least one patient. The AbioCor™ heart will likely undergo different stages of testing before it can be commercially sold. In the meantime, Abiomed, Inc. is working on a smaller version of the AbioCor™ heart.

Pennsylvania State University researchers had also been developing a complete artificial heart. In September 2000, Abiomed, Inc., acquired the rights to the Penn State Heart. Abiomed and Penn State's College of Medicine will work together to continue developing the device.

Several heart-assist devices are also undergoing various stages of testing. The Kantrowitz Cardio-Vad™, developed by Dr. Adrian Kantrowitz, is the only device that allows a patient to turn it on and off. Krantrowitz, the first U.S. surgeon to perform a heart transplant, spent thirty years fine-tuning the device. It is designed for patients with chronic (recurring) congestive heart failure who are not qualified for a heart transplant. It has three main parts—a pumping bladder weighing less than 1 ounce (about 28 grams), a couple of tubes leading from the pumping bladder (one for sending information to an attached computer and the other for inflating and deflating the bladder), and an external power source. The patient receives two power sources, a 5-pound, (2.3-kilogram) battery-powered unit and a unit the size of a small suitcase on wheels. Unlike other open-heart surgeries to implant heart devices, in which the breastbone is split open, the procedure to insert the CardioVad™ involves going through two ribs on the left chest. The device is sewn into the aorta, and a wire is run through the abdomen for linkage to the power source.

Smaller types of LVADs are also being tested. The *Jarvik-2000 Flowmaker*, invented by Dr. Robert Jarvik, the inventor of the first replacement heart, *Jarvik-7*, is about the size of a C battery. The small titanium turbine pump fits into the left ventricle and is powered by an external battery.

IMPROVING THE QUALITY OF LIFE

Researchers supported by the National Heart, Lung, and Blood Institute of the National Institutes of Health found, in a three-year study of patients with severe heart failure, that the use of a left ventricular assist device (LVAD) had helped extend the patients' lives. In addition, the medical device also improved their emotional state and physical function. These patients had been terminally ill and were ineligible for heart transplant due to their age or certain medical conditions.

Another small-sized LVAD has been invented by Dr. Michael DeBakey, Dr. George Noon (1934–), and NASA (National Aeronautics and Space Administration) engineers. Borrowing from space technology, the MicroMed DeBakey Ventricular Assist Device™ uses very light materials and computer chips. It weighs less than 4 ounces (113 grams) and has a simple moving part called the inducer-impeller. The titanium device, about the size of a walnut, plugs into the left ventricle and is powered by an external battery, connected by an inner-ear implant attached to the skull.

For More Information

Books

Berger, Melvin. *The Artificial Heart.* New York, NY: Franklin Watts, 1987.

Yount, Lisa. "From Sausage Casings to Six-Million-Dollar People." In *Medical Technology.* New York, NY: Facts On File, Inc., 1998.

Periodicals

Rose, Eric A. et al. "Long-Term Use of a Left Ventricular Assist Device for End-Stage Heart Failure." *The New England Journal of Medicine* (November 15, 2001): pp. 1435–1443.

Westaby, Stephen et al. "First Permanent implant of the Jarvik 2000 Heart." *The Lancet* (September 9, 2000): pp. 900–905.

Web Sites

"Affairs of the Heart." *Public Broadcasting System.* http://www.pbs.org/saf/1104/features/substitute.htm (accessed on July 22, 2002).

"The Heart: An Online Exploration." *The Franklin Institute Online.* http://sln.fi.edu/biosci/heart.html (accessed on July 22, 2002).

"Heartmate® Implantable Pneumatic Left Ventricular Assist System." *Texas Heart Institute.* http://www.bcm.tmc.edu/tmc/thi/iplvas.html (accessed on July 22, 2002).

Ballpoint Pen

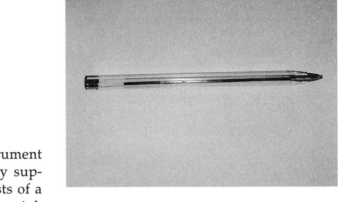

A ballpoint pen is a writing instrument with a tip that is continuously supplied with ink. The pen consists of a metal ball seated in a socket below an ink reservoir (the chamber or tube that holds a supply of ink). The ink reservoir is called an ink cartridge. When applied to a writing surface, the ball rotates and is bathed with just enough ink for smooth writing.

The ballpoint pen was developed as a solution to the problems of using a fountain pen for writing. Fountain pens need constant refilling with ink. The ink may leak or clog up the pen. The ballpoint pen, on the other hand, has its own ink supply which uses capillary action (a liquid's rising action through a tube) to keep the ink from leaking out. A freely rotating ball at the tip of the pen sits on a socket. The part that is used for writing is exposed, while the rest stays inside the pen. When the pen tip is applied to a writing surface, the ball rolls, transferring ink from the ink reservoir to the writing surface. Another advantage of the ballpoint pen is that its ink is quick-drying.

Different designs of ballpoint pens are available; however, they share common components (parts), including the ball, a point, ink, an ink reservoir, and an outer housing. Some pens have caps, while others have a retractable system that exposes the pen point or retracts it (draws it back) when a button on top of the pen is pushed.

Some ballpoint pens have multiple ink cartridges that enable the user to have different colored inks in one pen. Other pens have refillable ink cartridges. Other types can be used in space, underwater, or over grease.

Although the first patent for the ballpoint pen was granted in 1888, it took almost sixty years for the pen to be commercially available.

Trials and errors

In 1888, John J. Loud of Massachusetts obtained a patent for a pen with a rotating ball-tip that was constantly coated with ink by a reservoir above it. However, Loud and many others after him could not make the pen work because the ink either clogged the pen or leaked.

alloy: A mixture of a metal and a nonmetal or a mixture of two or more metals. For example, steel is an alloy made of the metal iron and the nonmetal carbon.

In the 1930s, two Hungarian brothers, Laszlo (1899–1985) and Georg Biro, developed a ballpoint pen using the thick ink used in printing newspapers. Laszlo had found that this type of ink dried fast. The brothers moved to Argentina during World War II (1939–45), and a company there produced the Biro pens. The English bought the right to produce the Biro pens for use by their Royal Air Force pilots after discovering that these pens did not leak at high altitudes. Soon after, the Biro pens became very popular in Europe.

brass: A yellowish metal that is an alloy of copper and zinc.

Fierce competition

die: Also called a die cast mold, a device used to shape materials by stamping or punching.

Ladislao (by which name Laszlo was now known) sold the U.S. rights to the Eversharp Company and Eberhard-Faber. However, a Chicago businessman, Milton Reynolds (1892–1976), beat them in marketing the Biro ballpoint pen. Reynolds, having acquired the pen on a visit to Argentina, copied the pen and sold it as Reynold's Rocket for the price of $12.50. Consumers soon realized that the pen did not perform as well as the manufacturer claimed. Sales dropped and Reynolds closed down his business. Other companies, including Papermate, Parker Pen Company,

The ballpoint pen has evolved into dozens of different colors and styles. *Photograph by Kelly A. Quin. Copyright © Kelly A. Quin. Reproduced by permission of the photographer.*

and A.T. Cross, came out with their versions of the ballpoint pen, which worked quite well.

At around the same time, in France, Baron Marcel Bich (1914–1994) started manufacturing BIC® pens (he had dropped the "h" from his name). By 1958, he had opened up business in the United States and sold ballpoint pens at the inexpensive price of 29 cents apiece. BIC® ballpoint pens continue to dominate the market.

Raw Materials

Several raw materials are used to make the components (parts) of a ballpoint pen. These include metals, plastics, and other chemicals. The original ballpoint pen had a steel ball. It has since been replaced by a textured tungsten carbide ball, which is less likely to lose its shape.

The ball is designed to be a perfect sphere that can grip almost any writing surface. The surface of the ball itself is made up of over 50,000

ink cartridge: The chamber or tube that sits on top of the ballpoint pen's metal ball and holds a supply of ink.

patent: A grant by a government to an inventor, assuring him or her the sole right to make and sell the invention for a period of time.

polished surfaces and pits (holes). The pits are connected by grooves that are continuous throughout the whole ball. This way, the ink is present not only on the surface of the ball but also inside the ball.

The point of the ballpoint pen is typically made of brass, an alloy (mixture) of copper and zinc. Brass is not only strong, it also has a pleasing appearance. It does not rust and can easily be formed to the desired shape. Brass may also be used to make the ink cartridge, the spring, or the body of the pen. The body of the pen is sometimes made of aluminum. Stainless steel may be used for pen components. Precious metals, such as gold, silver, or platinum, are used to plate more expensive pens, by which process a thin layer of one metal covers another metal. For example, a thin coating of gold may be applied over a brass pen.

Plastics have become popular raw materials for manufacturing ballpoint pens. They are rust-resistant, lightweight, easily formed, and inexpensive. Plastics are used to make the body of the pen, the ink cartridge, the push button, and part of the pen tip.

Ballpoint companies that make their own ink aim to make ink that is slightly thick, dries slowly in the pen reservoir, and is free of particles. These characteristics ensure the continuous flow of the ink for smooth writing. Various pigments and dyes are included in the ink formula to produce color. Other ingredients, including lubricants, surfactants, thickeners, and preservatives, are also added. These ingredients are usually mixed with castor oil, oleic acid, or sulfonamide plasticizer.

The Manufacturing Process

Ballpoint pens are made to order in great quantities. In advanced shops, pens are made from raw materials to finished products in less than five minutes. Manufacturers may differ slightly in the processes they use to make the pens; however, they generally follow the same basic steps.

Making the ink

1 Large batches of ink are made in a specific area of the manufacturing factory. Workers follow formula instructions for making the ink. Raw materials are poured into the batch tank and thoroughly mixed. Based on the formula used, these batches may be heated or cooled as necessary to blend the materials more quickly.

stamping: The process of shaping or cutting out material by forcing it into or against a mold.

2 Some of the raw materials that come in large quantities are added directly into the batch tank using computer-run controls. These controls, activated by the press of a button, add the materials in

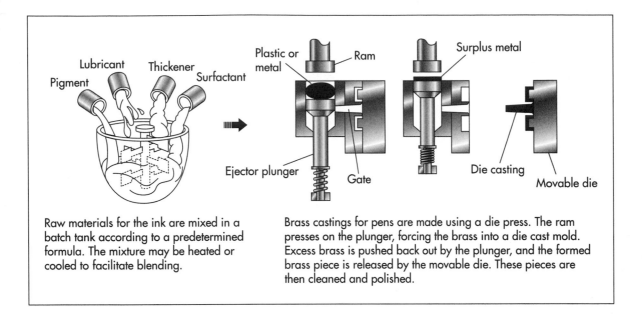

Raw materials for the ink are mixed in a batch tank according to a predetermined formula. The mixture may be heated or cooled to facilitate blending.

Brass castings for pens are made using a die press. The ram presses on the plunger, forcing the brass into a die cast mold. Excess brass is pushed back out by the plunger, and the formed brass piece is released by the movable die. These pieces are then cleaned and polished.

specified amounts. They also regulate the mixing speeds and amounts of heating and cooling. The ink is checked at different points during its manufacture.

Stamping and forming of pen components

3 An outside company typically supplies the tungsten carbide balls. Various molds are used to make the other parts of the pen, including the body and the point. Sheets of brass are automatically inserted into stamping machines, which cut out thousands of small discs. The metal discs are first softened and then poured into a compression chamber, which consists of a steel ram and an ejector plunger.

The ram presses on the plunger, which retracts (draws back), forcing the metal into a die cast mold (a device for forming the brass). The plunger pushes out the excess brass, while the movable die cast mold releases the formed pieces. These pieces make up the parts of the pen.

4 The formed pieces are put in a bath to remove oils used in the die-casting process. They are removed from the bath and cut to the measurements of the particular pen. Next, the pieces are polished and cleaned again to remove any remaining oils. The ball is then inserted into the cavity of the pen point.

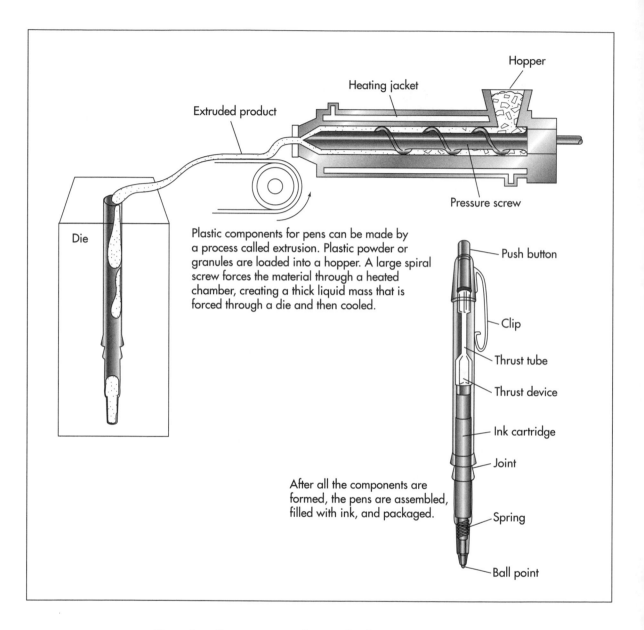

Hopper

Heating jacket

Extruded product

Die

Pressure screw

Plastic components for pens can be made by a process called extrusion. Plastic powder or granules are loaded into a hopper. A large spiral screw forces the material through a heated chamber, creating a thick liquid mass that is forced through a die and then cooled.

Push button

Clip

Thrust tube

Thrust device

Ink cartridge

Joint

Spring

Ball point

After all the components are formed, the pens are assembled, filled with ink, and packaged.

Forming the pen exterior and other parts

5 The plastic parts of the pen are made using the extrusion process or injection molding. In either case, the plastic materials come as granules or powder, which are placed into a large hopper (receptacle).

The extrusion process involves forcing the plastic granules or powder through a heated chamber with the help of a pressure screw. The resulting product—a thick, flowing mass—is forced through a die. The formed plastic piece is allowed to cool and cut. Pieces, such the pen body and ink reservoir, are made using this method.

Injection molding is used for pieces that have a more complicated form. These include the caps, ends, and mechanical components. In this process, the plastic granules or powder is heated. With the help of high pressure, the liquid plastic is forced into the molds, filling them. The plastic is allowed to cool and harden. The formed solid plastics are then released from the die.

Ink filling and assembly

6 After the parts that would make up the ballpoint pen are made, assembly takes place. Typically, the ballpoint is attached to the ink reservoir. The pieces are transported by conveyor belt to injectors, machines that fill the ink reservoir with the specific colored ink. If a spring is going to be part of the pen, it is placed on the barrel of the reservoir.

Final assembly, packaging, and shipping

7 The pen point and ink reservoir are placed inside the body of the pen. Other parts, including the caps and ends, are added. Other finishing steps, such as final cleaning or the addition of coatings or decorations, are also done.

The finished pens are packaged according to how they will be sold. Single pens are put into blister packages with cardboard backings. Groups of pens are packed into bags or boxes. These are then put into boxes, stacked on pallets (movable platforms), and shipped to distributors.

Quality Control

The quality of the pen components is checked throughout all the manufacturing steps. Since thousands of parts are produced each day, it is not possible to inspect each piece. Line inspectors check random samples visually. They also perform other, stricter tests, including length measurements of pen parts, and the condition of surface coatings.

Quality control of the batches of ink is also conducted. After all the ingredients are added to the batch, a sample is tested at the laboratory. Physical and chemical testings are done. If a batch does not meet standards, adjustments to the ingredients are made. For example, colors can be adjusted by adding more dyes.

In addition to the specific tests, line inspectors at each manufacturing stage check the components as they are made and look for things such as misshapen pens, inadequately filled ink reservoirs, and incorrectly assembled parts. Some finished products are also tested to make sure the pens write correctly.

The Future

The ballpoint pen remains a very popular writing instrument. Continuing research focuses on better pen grip for writing comfort, as well as on longer-lasting inks. Manufacturers also constantly come up with new barrel (the cylindrical housing) ideas, including futuristic designs and pastels that are especially popular with younger people. A new type of ballpoint pen, equipped with a battery, has a built-in light that allows for use in the dark.

Manufacturers will continue to develop processes that use metals and plastics requiring very little processing. This means little waste during production, increased manufacturing speed, and lower cost of the final products.

For more Information

Books

Gostony, Henry, and Schneider, Stuart L. *The Incredible Ball Point Pen*. Atglen, PA: Schiffer Publishing Limited, 1998.

Periodicals

Rigby, Rhymer. "Inventor whose fame is writ large." *Management Today*. (March 1998): p. 104.

Web Sites

"The Battle of the Ballpoint Pens." *Inventors*. http://inventors.miningco.com/library/weekly/aa101697.htm (accessed July 22, 2002).

"BIC®: How It's Made." *BIC® World USA*. http://www.bicworldusa.com/inter_us/stationery/how_is_made/index.asp (accessed on July 22, 2002).

"A Brief History of Writing Instruments." *Inventors*. http://inventors.miningco.com/library/weekly/aa100197.htm (accessed July 22, 2002).

Bean Bag Plush Toy

A bean bag plush toy is an soft, stuffed, hand-sized animal toy filled with bean-like plastic pellets and fiberfill (material used for pillow stuffing). The original nine Beanie Babies® created by H. Ty Warner in 1993 started a "fad" that has continued to last and has renewed interest in other bean bag plush toys.

Bean bag ancestors

Bean bags are among the oldest toys and have been made in various shapes and forms. Some have taken on simple geometric shapes, while others are made into animal and doll forms. For centuries, they have been filled with beans, peas, rice, or pebbles.

A cousin to bean bag toys is the rag doll, which has also been around for many years. People have probably made rag dolls for their children since the first fabrics were woven. Like bean bag dolls and animals, they have been toted around by children and brought to bed for comfort and companionship. Rags are the stuffing used in many old dolls with cloth bodies and heads made from china, ceramic, or porcelain.

Bean bag plush toys are not filled with beans. Their soft stuffing consists of small bean-like plastic pellets and polyester fiberfill.

Seven of the nine original Beanie Babies introduced in 1993: (top) Patti the Platypus, Flash the Dolphin, Splash the Whale, Squealer the Pig; (bottom) Pinchers the Lobster, Brownie the Bear (later named Cubbie the Bear), and Legs the Frog. Missing are Chocolate the Moose and Spot the Dog. *Photograph by Kelly A. Quin. Copyright © Kelly A. Quin. Reproduced by permission of the photographer.*

assembly line: A line of factory workers and equipment through which a product that is being put together passes from one operation to another until completion.

collectible: One of a group of a certain object that is sought after by a collector.

Bears remain very popular toys in the United States, perhaps because people associate them with the classic teddy bear toy that was created in honor of President Theodore "Teddy" Roosevelt (1858–1919) in 1903. These stuffed creatures continue to have a sentimental value and have become the most popular bean bag plush toys.

Birth of the Beanie Babies®

H. Ty Warner (1944–) is the genius behind the Beanie Babies®. For eighteen years, Warner worked for Dakin, Inc., a major stuffed toy maker, before forming Ty Inc. in Oakbrook, Illinois, in 1986. He developed Beanie Babies® with the idea of marketing small, cuddly plush toys that children can hold in their hands and that they can afford to buy using their allowance money. He also wanted the toys to be soft and not stiff like the other stuffed animals in the market. Therefore, to make the toys soft and posable, he understuffed them with bean-like plastic pellets and fiberfill.

In November 1993, Warner debuted the first nine Beanie Babies® at the World Toy Fair in New York City. In early 1994, he began selling them in small stores across Illinois. In June 1994, Ty Inc. introduced thirty-six new Beanie Babies®, and soon the hand-sized plush toys had found their way to the southern states. Sales steadily rose as the plush toys attracted not only children but also adults. Before long, Beanie Babies® became collectibles, starting a buying frenzy across the United States. By 1996, over 100 million Beanie Babies® had been sold.

It's all in the marketing

Since the mid-1990s, the Beanie Babies® "fad" has grown. Apart from endearing designs, Ty Inc. employed several clever marketing tactics to increase its sales. Unlike other toys that are mass-produced, varieties of Beanie Babies® have limited production. Once consumers realized a certain number of toys were being "retired" (discontinued) periodically, they would snap up new releases as soon as the products hit the stores.

In 1996, Ty Inc. launched a Web site where, among other things, soon-to-be-retired toys were announced. Collectors would then quickly buy up the potential "retirees," thus creating instant collectibles. By 1997, the company was discontinuing and creating new Beanie Babies® every four to six months. When Ty Inc. announced that it would retire all Beanie Babies® by December 31, 1999, consumers not only protested but went on a buying streak.

As stated before, Beanie Babies® appealed not only to children but also to adults. Adults who shop at specialty stores, such as flower shops and hotel gift shops, became collectors overnight, thus opening up a whole new market. And since the price was reasonable—between $4 and $7—they were more likely to buy several.

Other gimmicks, such as creating "generations" of hang tags and tush tags, further enhanced the toys' appeal, especially to collection hunters. Each toy has two tags. The hang tag, also called a swing tag or a heart tag because of its heart shape, identifies the toy by name and birth date. Those made after 1996 include a poem describing the animal's habits or character. The second tag, called a tush tag, shows the toy contents, the manufacturing location, company trademark and registration.

fiberfill: A synthetic material used for stuffing pillows and other products.

pile: Loops of yarn that form the surface of some fabrics.

polyvinyl chloride (PVC): A type of plastic that is resistant to moisture and weathering.

Corporate America joins the craze

In 1997, McDonald's Corporation added to the Beanie Babies® craze by including miniature versions of existing Beanie Babies® with its Happy Meals. The first Teenie Beanie Babies™ promotion featured ten toys to be released two per week during a five-week period. The promotion lasted just two weeks because the supply of 100 million toys had been exhausted.

Design

Designing a bean bag plush toy begins with a prototype (a standard model) that may take several years to complete. In the case of Beanie Babies®, Ty Warner designs the toys by making several prototypes of the same design. Warner varies the shapes, colors, materials, features, and accessories (additional features) on each prototype, and then asks for friends' and employees' opinions to select the best design. During the design process, changes continue to be made not only to the toy itself but also in its name, tags, and the poem on the hang tag. Even after a toy has been in the market, changes may be made to improve it.

At SWIBCO, another plush toy manufacturer, the Puffkins® Collectibles undergo the same process. These plush toys have rounded shapes; therefore, some types of animals, such as snakes or long-legged birds, are not suited to the design. The design idea may come from employees. (In fact, an employee contest resulted in the Puffkins® name.) Other design ideas may come from children, Puffkins® collectors, or the general public.

SWIBCO's art department creates up to six designs, and the sketches are reviewed by the firm's owners. From the sketches, factory workers produce handmade prototypes, using different fabric and color combinations. The owners may approve the prototypes for manufacture or request new designs. Of the original six designs, four may be manufactured. The two that are not selected may be revised and kept for future use. The art department may review these designs later and get fresh ideas from them.

Raw Materials

Bean bag plush toys are not filled with beans. Their characteristic soft stuffing consists of small bean-like plastic pellets and polyester fiberfill. The plastic pellets are made of either polyvinyl chloride (PVC) or polyethylene (PE), and are produced by specialty suppliers. The polyester fiberfill is the stuffing commonly used for pillows, comforters, some furniture, and many other products.

A young girl hugs her favorite Beanie Babies® toy, one of the must-have toys in the mid- and late 1990s. *Photograph by Kelly A. Quin. Copyright © Kelly A. Quin. Reproduced by permission of the photographer.*

The outer fabric of the toy is made of synthetic (artificial) plush. The fabric called plush typically has a soft nap, the term used to describe the short fibers that stick out from the fabric surface to give it a smooth, soft feel.

Manufacturers usually use unique fabrics to distinguish their products from others of almost similar characteristics. For example, SWIBCO uses high-pile fabric for a fluffy, furry appearance. Ty Inc., on the other hand, created its own synthetic fabric called Tylon for use with Beanie Babies®.

The eyes, noses, and other hard plastic features of bean bag plush toys are made by an outside specialty manufacturer. The parts are all childproof, which means that they cannot be easily removed or broken. The eyes are placed onto plastic stems, and the stems are passed through the fabric to be securely attached with fasteners on the fabric back. Some manufacturers use eyes and other features made from felt material. These felt parts may be produced by an outside supplier and then sewn on at the manufacturing factory. Some manufacturers create eyes and noses on the fabric itself by stitching layers of thread by machine to produce the desired look.

Yarn and thread are used for insect antennas and cat whiskers. Large body parts, such as legs, feet, beaks, wings, and ears, are made of plush or other fabric. These body parts are usually stuffed with filling. Ribbons that are used are high-quality, double-sided satin.

Bean bag plush toys generally have one or two tags, or strips of material attached to the finished products. The tags may carry the manufacturer's name, location, and telephone number; toy contents; washing instructions; and the ages of children for whom the toy is intended. For Beanie Babies®, two tags are used. The hang tag is printed on paper and carries the manufacturer's identification and information about the animal character. It is attached to the toy with a plastic strip fastener made of red or white clear plastic. Each fastener is about 0.5 to 0.74 inch (1.3 to 1.9 centimeters) long. The fabric safety tag, also called the tush tag, is attached to the animal's hindquarters. The tush tag shows the contents of the toy, its name, its place of manufacture, and registration and trademark information. To prevent the making of counterfeits (fake products), the tush tag also sports a morphing hologram (a changing three-dimensional image). Ty Inc. periodically changes the design of these tags.

The Manufacturing Process

The large-scale production of bean bag plush toys is done on an assembly line, in which specific parts of the toy are made at different sewing-machine stations, then moved to the end of the line for final assembly and stuffing.

Making the pattern

1 The pattern made from the selected prototype is computer-generated to fit a certain length and width of fabric. The resulting patterns are then laid out on the fabric, making sure that very little fabric is wasted.

Producing the formed animals

2 Cutting dies (molds) are also computer-generated from the pattern information to produce the form for each part of the toy animal. Using the different dies, parts of the toy are stamped out (cut by

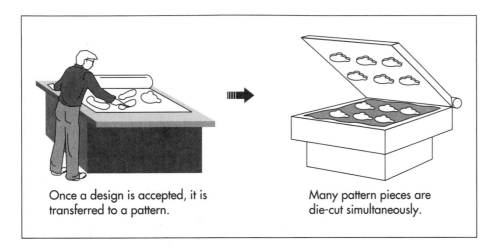

Once a design is accepted, it is transferred to a pattern.

Many pattern pieces are die-cut simultaneously.

Plush toy patterns and their corresponding cutting dies are computer-generated to maximize efficiency and minimize the amount of waste fabric. Multiple layers of plush fabric are simultaneously cut with dies.

using high pressure) of multiple layers of plush fabric. Some toy parts may also be hand-cut.

Assembling the face features

3 Each animal's face and body parts with accessory attachments are assembled first. The eyes and nose are fastened into place with a special hand tool. Whiskers, antennas, and other features made of yarn and thread are sewn in place.

Sewing the animal parts

4 At long rows of sewing stations called an assembly line, sewers stitch parts of the toy animal together. Industrial sewing machines, which are powerful machines suited for large-scale production, are used. However, the machine parts are especially made for sewing small pieces of fabric.

The sewing is done on the back sides of two matching fabric pieces. One sewing station may be responsible for sewing just the ears. Another station sews the paws, while still another is responsible for the head. At other stations farther along the assembly line, body parts and the tags are attached to the main body until the whole animal is completely assembled. Manufacturers vary in the placement of the tags on the animal's body. For Beanie Babies®, just the tush tags are attached. Then the animal is turned right-side out.

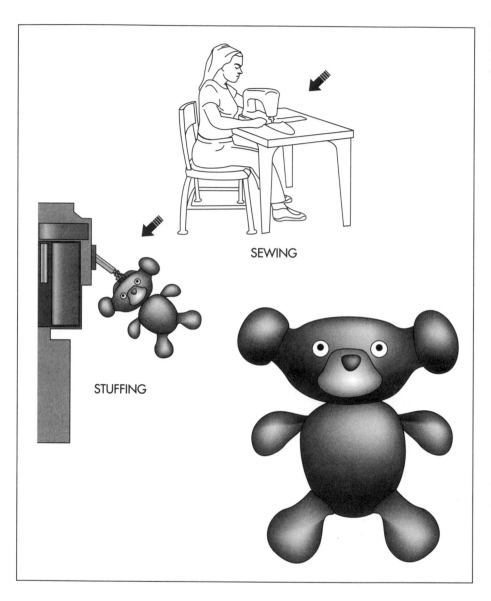

SEWING

STUFFING

Pattern pieces are sewn together by seamstresses. Once sewn, the plush body is turned right-side out and stuffed with fiberfill and PVC pellets. Stuffing is accomplished both by machine and by hand.

Stuffing the animal

5 Depending on the manufacturer, fiberfill may be added to certain pieces, such as the legs, before attachment to the body. The plastic pellets and fiberfill are measured before they are machine-stuffed

into the animal to ensure a uniform weight and to give the toy an under-stuffed feel. Assemblers also subject the toy to a touch and squeeze test to make sure it will sit on the hand, bend at the legs, and feel cuddly. The last of the filling is stuffed by hand, and the opening in the head or side seam is sewn by hand.

Adding the final accessories and packaging

6 Neck ribbons and other final details are tied in place. At this stage, Beanie Babies® hang tags are clipped on with plastic fasteners. The toys are sent to the packaging department where they are bagged and boxed for shipment.

Quality Control

The sewers and assemblers make sure the toy animals are put together properly and that they are filled with appropriately measured stuffing. Before packaging, the toys are rechecked. When the toys reach the distribution centers in the United States or other parts of the world, they are inspected before they are repackaged for shipment to retail stores.

The Future

Although some observers predicted that the market for Beanie Babies® and other bean bag plush toys would soon decline, the popularity of these toys continues. Clubs that have been formed by collectors are as active as ever and have various Internet sites with contents ranging from new products to counterfeit reports and helpful tips. Children are not the only ones buying the toys. Adults of all ages, including men, are collecting them. Many are willing to pay several more times the original price of around $4 to $7 to acquire toys that have been retired (no longer manufactured).

Bean bag toy manufacturers have created elaborate Web sites to fuel the bean bag toy craze. Fans can find out about toys that are soon to be released and discontinued, as well as post their questions and complaints. Some fans have even created their own Internet sites to share their experiences with these toys.

Bean bag toy fans claim the demand will last for many more years. Secondary markets (places other than retail stores or wholesale firms, which ordinarily sell the toys), including Internet auction sites, sports card shops, and florists, now carry these toys. People trying to cash in on the fad have written books from any angle they can think of. Some have published monthly magazines, while other have developed software programs targeting collectors. Also joining the many businesses are individuals offering authentication services to help establish that a certain toy is the real thing.

Many products marketed as beanies have flooded the market, including cartoon characters, sports stars, and entertainment figures. A recent concept of bean bag plush toys is taking advantage of children's interest in computers. The four-inch, plush PuterBabies®, who go by such technology names as Byte the dog and Bandwidth the Raccoon, are designed to sit on computer monitors. It seems as if bean bag plush toys will be here for a while.

For More Information

Books

Boardman, Doug and Bernadette. *Beanie Babies®: Behind the Boom.* Nashua, NH: 38th Street Publishing, 1998.

Phillips, Becky, and Becky Estenssoro. *Beanie Mania II: The Complete Collector's Guide.* Naperville, IL: Dinomates, Inc., 1998.

Periodicals

Mannix, Margaret, and James M. Pethokoukis. "Beanie Bubble." *U.S. News & World Report* (August 3, 1998): pp. 53–58.

Morice, Laura. "Still Bonkers Over Beanies." *Good Housekeeping* (July 1999): p. 104.

Web Sites

aboutbeanies.com. http://www.aboutbeanies.com (accessed July 22, 2002).

Brereton, Erin. "Beanie Babies® Background Information." *Beanie Buddy.* http://www.beanie-buddy.com/history.html (accessed on July 22, 2002).

Welcome to PuterBabies: Make Your Computer Their Home. http://www.cybergetic.com/~puterbabies/ (accessed July 22, 2002).

Black Box

"Black box" is a term used to describe the computerized recording equipment carried by modern commercial aircraft. The black box set typically consists of the flight data recorder (FDR) and the cockpit voice recorder (CVR). Each recorder is about the size of a shoe box, has reflective strips, and is bright orange in color. No one is exactly sure why the recorders are called black boxes. Some say the term was coined because the boxes are usually burned to a blackish color when retrieved at a crash site. Others believe the term is used because most electronic equipment in an airplane is housed in black boxes.

Some say the term black box was coined because the box is burned to a blackish color when it is retrieved at the crash site.

The FDR tracks a variety of data about the flight of the airplane, such as airspeed, altitude, and heading (the direction in which the aircraft is traveling). The CVR records radio transmissions and sounds in the cockpit, such as the flight crew's conversations, engine noises and warnings, and landing gear extension and retraction. Although the boxes are constructed to withstand fire, water, and tremendous impact, they are stored in the airplane tail section, the part that is most crash-survivable. In the event of an accident, information stored in these black boxes can help determine its cause.

Searching for the right black box

Wilbur (1867–1912) and Orville (1871–1948) Wright carried the first black box during one of their initial flights in the early1900s in their hometown of Dayton, Ohio. The crude device recorded the length of flight,

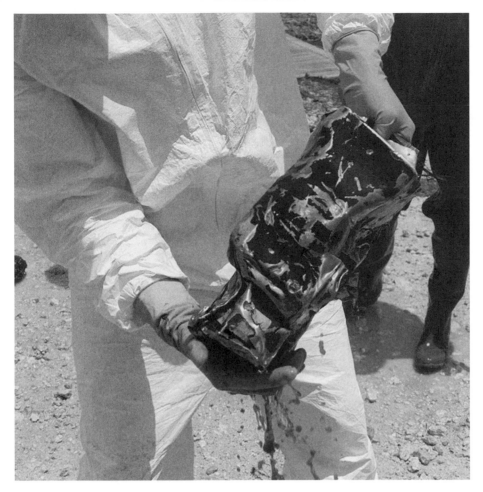

Beaten, smashed, and water-logged, the black box can survive almost any crash and the cockpit voice recording that is part of it can provide vital clues about what went wrong during the final moments of a flight. *Reproduced by permission of AP/Wide World Photos.*

altitude: Height above the Earth's surface.

gravity: The force that pulls objects down toward the Earth.

heading: The direction in which an aircraft is traveling.

memory chip: Also called microchip, a very small piece of silicon that carries interconnected electronic components.

shelf life: The length of time a battery may be stored before it starts losing its effectiveness.

sonar: A system that uses transmitted and reflected underwater sound waves to determine the location of a submerged object.

speed, and propeller rotation. Charles Lindbergh (1902–1974), the first person to make a nonstop solo flight across the Atlantic Ocean in 1927, also used a black box during his many flights. His black box consisted of a bar graph that marked changes in barometric pressure using ink on paper wrapped around a rotating drum.

In the early 1940s, with the increasing popularity of commercial flight, the Civil Aeronautics Board (CAB; now the Federal Aviation Administration, or FAA) concluded that there should be a reliable way to record flight data. After a series of airplane crashes occurred in the late 1940s, the CAB required that the aircraft industry look into ways of preserving its record of flight in the event of a crash. Early attempts at inventing a black box consisted of a stylus (a pointed instrument) that cut images into black paper coated with white lacquer and a device that used magnetic tape. A magnetic tape is a plastic tape coated with iron oxide for use in recording. However, these devices were never used.

The proper black box

It was not until 1948 that black box technology was developed. Professor James J. Ryan (1914–1973) of the University of Minnesota invented what he called the *VGA Flight Recorder*. The device was about the size of a breadbox and weighed 10 pounds (4.5 kilograms). It had two separate compartments. One compartment contained the measuring devices (the altimeter, the accelerometer, and the airspeed indicator), and the other held the recording device, which connected to the three instruments. The black box recorded flight information on aluminum tape. The device was encased in two steel containers, with about an inch of insulation in between. In 1951, the General Mills engineering department decided to fund Ryan's invention. Ryan's basic design is still used in black boxes today, although it has undergone numerous improvements.

In 1958, the CAB required commercial aircraft registered in the United States to have an approved flight data recorder on board. One single strip of aluminum foil recorded between 200 to 400 hours of data. A stylus literally scratched markings on the moving foil. In 1965, the CVR was added, and the recorders were painted orange or bright yellow so they could be easily located after a crash. In FDRs, the stylus-type recording was replaced with a .25-inch (6.4 millimeters) Mylar® magnetic tape.

Improved black boxes

In the 1970s, the FDRs began having problems handling the increasing volume of data being transmitted by the sensors. As a result, the flight data acquisition unit (FDAU) was introduced to act as middleman between the sensors and the FDR. The FDAU processed the data received from the sensors and then passed the data on to the FDR. The FDR magnetic tape recorded about twenty-five hours of data. However, the FDR tapes were found to be vulnerable to intense fire and impact shock. By early 1990, the magnetic tape was replaced by digital memory chips.

Just as the recording time has increased, the number of parameters the black box tracks has also grown—from about three or four to more than three hundred parameters. The parameters refer to the different pieces of information relating to the aircraft, such as the airspeed, altitude, vertical acceleration, heading, the time of each radio transmission to the air traffic control, cockpit conversations, and radio communications. As of 2002, the FAA required commercial aircraft to record twenty-eight parameters.

Perhaps the most significant advance in black box manufacture has been the improvement in its construction, allowing it to withstand the tremendous force of a crash. Early recorders withstood about 100 g's (100 times the force of gravity), which is similar to being dropped from a height of about 10 feet (3 meters) onto a concrete surface. This figure was increased to 1,000 g's and then to 3,400 g's.

Design

The flight data recorder and the cockpit voice recorder have the same components (parts). Both have a power supply, a memory unit, electronic controller board, and a signal beacon.

Power supply

The black box gets its power supply from two generators, which in turn are powered by the plane's engines. One generator provides a power source of 28-volt DC (direct current), while the second generator has a power source of 115-volt AC (alternating current). The dual voltage allows the black boxes to be used in a variety of aircraft. The black box also has a battery that can run for thirty continuous days. The battery has a six-year shelf life.

Crash-survivable memory unit (CSMU)

The CSMU is designed to store twenty-five hours of digital (using computer memory chips) flight information. The stored information is of high quality because the memory chips can hold a huge amount of information in its original form.

Integrated controller and circuitry board (ICB)

The ICB contains the electronic circuitry that acts as a switchboard for the incoming data.

Interface

The interface, as its name implies, serves as the connection for the input devices from which the black boxes obtain information about the aircraft. The FDR interface receives and processes signals from aircraft instruments, such as the airspeed indicator, on-board warning alarms, and the altimeter (the instrument that measures altitude).

Black boxes help NTSB investigators determine the cause of crashes like this one in Dania Beach, Florida, in January 2002.
Reproduced by permission of AP/Wide World Photos.

The CVR interface receives and processes signals from microphones found in the cockpit, including in the headsets of the two pilots and possibly of another crew member, as well as on the overhead instrument panel between the two pilots. The microphones pick up the conversations between the cockpit crew and between the cockpit and ground crews. Communications with air-traffic controllers and radio weather briefings are also collected and stored by the CVR. In addition, the microphones track engine noise, stall warnings, landing gear extension and retraction, and other sounds in the immediate surroundings.

Underwater locator beacon (ULB)

The cylindrical ULB, which also functions as the handle for picking up the black box, helps investigators identify its location in the event of

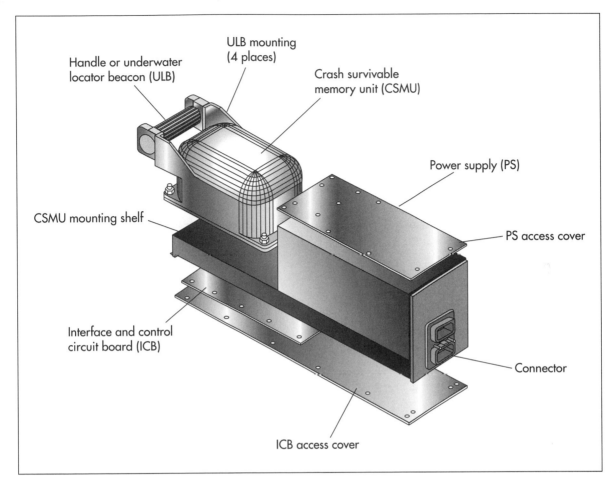

The flight data recorder (FDR) is a miniaturized computer system that tracks a variety of data regarding the flight of the airplane, including its airspeed, position, and altitude.

an over-water accident. A submerger sensor in the ULB activates it when water touches that sensor. The ULB is called a "pinger" because, once it is activated, it makes a pinging sound once every second. It can transmit sound from as deep as 14,000 feet (4,267 meters) that can be detected by sonar. The ULB can make the pinging sound for thirty days.

The Manufacturing Process

The key components (the power supply, the interface and control circuit board, and the memory chip circuits) are constructed as separate units and then assembled to create the black box unit. This way, if one component needs replacing, the whole black box does not have to be taken apart.

Insulation for memory circuit board

1 Special attention is given to protecting the memory chip circuits since they will store the data that would be helpful to investigators in the event of an aircraft accident. Several layers of materials house the memory boards. The outermost housing is typically made of stainless steel, although some manufacturers may use titanium.

2 Underneath the stainless steel shell is a layer of insulation, followed by a thick slab of paraffin, which forms a thermal block. If fire occurs during an aircraft accident, the paraffin melts and absorbs the heat, thereby helping maintain a lower temperature for the memory board found underneath the paraffin.

3 Next comes another layer of paraffin thermal block and, finally, another layer of insulation. The whole insulation assembly is mounted on a steel plate, which can be removed to access the memory board.

Attaching the CSMU, the interface, and the ICB to the mounting shelf

4 Using four large bolts, the finished crash-survivable memory unit (CSMU) is fastened onto the front of a heavy metal-plate mounting shelf. The power supply is attached behind the CSMU.

5 The interface and the control circuit board are attached by screws to the underside of the mounting shelf. A metal protector cover, which also provides easy access, is placed over the board.

Attaching the ULB

6 The underwater locator beacon (ULB) is attached to the two arms that extend from the memory unit. The ULB is a cylinder that also serves as the handle for the black box. If the black box is sold without the ULB, the manufacturer attaches a hollow metal tube in its place. Then, the user installs the ULB.

Painting the outer casing

7 The outer casing is painted orange or bright yellow to make it more visible in case of a crash. Reflective strips are also applied.

Rescuers recover the flight data recorder, or "black box," from the wreckage of a plane crash in the Philippines that killed all 131 passengers on board. *Reproduced by permission of AP/Wide World Photos.*

Quality Control

Black boxes have to survive a crash so that the information they contain can be recovered by investigators. For this reason, manufacturers have to comply with federal regulations by subjecting the box to grueling testing measures that mimic catastrophic crash conditions. The simulated crash conditions are usually in excess of what the black box would experience in an actual crash.

To make sure the black box will survive the initial impact of a crash, it is fired from an air cannon toward an aluminum wall, hitting the wall at 3,400 times its weight. According to experts, this figure is equivalent to or more than the force of impact the black box would experience in an actual crash.

A piercing test involves dropping, from a height of ten feet (three meters), a 500-pound (227-kilogram) weight with an attached one-quarter-inch steel pin onto the black box. The box also undergoes a crushing pressure of 5,000 pounds (2,270 kilograms).

Since most aircraft accidents involve fire, the black box is cooked at 2,012 degrees Fahrenheit (1,100 degrees Celsius) for one hour, the temperature at which aviation fuel burns. The black box is also submerged under the equivalent of 20,000 feet (6,000 miles) of seawater for thirty days. Other tests include submersion in aviation fuel, lubricants, toilet-flushing liquid, and fire-extinguisher substances. Vibration tests are also performed.

Federal regulations require that flight data recorders for new commercial aircraft record twenty-eight parameters. The black boxes are designed to be maintenance-free, and the average time between failures should be greater than 15,000 hours.

The Future

A new black box design combines the FDR and the CVR. This type of black box has been used in military fighter craft and helicopters. This new unit is lightweight and takes up less space, while at the same time storing the same amount of information. It has been proposed that, since this design is available, an aircraft can have two of these combined black boxes, one to be stored at the usual location at the airplane's tail section, and the second one, near the cockpit. In addition, authorities are also studying the possibility of video recordings in light of recent advances in video technology.

A solution being proposed to preserve flight data during a crash involves a black box called a deployable flight incident recorder (DFIR). The device is designed to automatically bail out from a crashing aircraft and "fly away" from the accident site. This technology, which has been used in military planes and helicopters for over three decades, is quite expensive. The manufacturer, DRS Technologies, Inc., is developing the next-generation DFIR for the military, a design that takes into consideration the safety regulations and cost for commercial aircraft.

For More Information

Periodicals

"A Passion for Safety: Professor James 'Crash' Ryan." *ME News* (Winter 2000): pp. 6–7.

Web Sites

"Cockpit Voice Recorders (CVR) and Flight Data Recorders (FDR)." *National Transportation Safety Board.* http://www.ntsb.gov/Aviation/CVR_FDR.htm (accessed on July 22, 2002).

"Flight-Data Recorders: Orange Is Good, Black Is Bad." *EDN Access.* http:www.e-insite.net/ednmag/contents/images/178107.pdf (accessed on July 22, 2002).

"The 'Wright' Stuff." *Federal Aviation Administration.* http://www.faa.gov/education/wright/wright.htm (accessed on July 22, 2002).

Cereal

Photograph by Kelly A. Quin. Copyright © Kelly A. Quin. Reproduced by permission of the photographer.

Ready-to-eat cereals are served in nine out of ten American households.

ereal is a grain food eaten as a main course for breakfast and is typically served with milk or cream. Some cereals, such as oatmeal, require a few minutes of cooking. Other hot cereals, called "instant," can be prepared in less time. Cold, ready-to-eat cereal, on the other hand, can be eaten right out of the package.

A healthy start

Cold, ready-to-eat breakfast cereals developed because of religious beliefs. In 1829, American clergyman and vegetarian Sylvester Graham (1794–1851) invented the graham cracker. Made from coarsely ground whole wheat flour, the graham cracker was part of a vegetarian diet he developed to cure intemperance (excessive intake of alcoholic drinks).

In the 1860s, influenced by Graham, Seventh-Day Adventists, who believed that healthy living included eating the right kinds of food, established the Western Health Reform Institute in Battle Creek, Michigan, later renamed the Battle Creek Sanitarium. John Harvey Kellogg (1852–1943), the head physician at the institute, invented a product called Granola, made from wheat, oats, and corn that had been mixed, baked, and coarsely ground. In 1894, Kellogg and his brother Will Keith (better known as W.K., 1860–1951) produced the first precooked flaked cereal made of wheat. They called the cereal Granose. This product was the predecessor of Kellogg's Corn Flakes®.

Bowls of healthful, non-sugary cereals like Rice Chex® have proven to be a good way to give a person extra energy in the morning while also helping the heart. *Photograph by Kelly A. Quin. Copyright © Kelly A. Quin. Reproduced by permission of the photographer.*

In 1895, C.W. (Charles William) Post (1854–1914), John Kellogg's patient, started his own cereal business with the introduction of Postum® cereal coffee, an "un-caffeinated" beverage advertised as a health food. Two years later, he produced a ready-to-eat cold cereal called Grape-Nuts®, named after the ingredient grape sugar and the cereal's nutty flavor. This was soon followed by a corn flake cereal called Post Toasties®.

Kellogg's and Post's success led many others to open cereal factories, but those businesses quickly failed. The success of the two cereal pioneers was partly the result of clever advertisements that presented their healthful cereals as quick, convenient, and tasty breakfast foods. To this day, Kellogg and Post cereals continue to be consumed by the American public. Ready-to-eat cereals are served in nine out of ten American households. Flaked cereals make up about one-third of ready-to-eat cereal sales.

antioxidant: A substance that prevents food from discoloring or going stale.

bran: The outer coat of a cereal grain.

conveyor belt: A continuous moving belt that transports objects from one place to another.

Raw Materials

Grain is the most important raw material in any breakfast cereal. The grains most commonly used are corn, wheat, oats, rice, and barley. Most cereals contain other ingredients, including salt, yeast, sweeteners, flavoring agents, coloring agents, vitamins, minerals, and preservatives. Some cereals, such as oatmeal (usually served hot) and shredded wheat, contain no additional ingredients.

The sweeteners used in cereals include malt extract (a sweet substance made from barley), white sugar, brown sugar, corn syrup, honey, and molasses. Some natural cereals are sweetened with concentrated fruit juice. Flavors, such as chocolate, cinnamon, and fruit may be added. Nuts, dried fruit, and marshmallows may also be added.

Vitamins and minerals that are lost during cooking are added. The most important is Vitamin B1, most of which is destroyed by heat. To prevent cereals from discoloring and becoming stale and rancid, the antioxidants BHA and BHT are added as preservatives.

The Manufacturing Process

Ready-to-eat breakfast cereals may come in the form of flaked, puffed, and shredded cereals. Some have been formed into particular shapes, such as circles or letters. Others come mixed with other ingredients, including nuts, dried fruits, and flavors.

Preparing the grain

corn grits: Coarsely ground corn.

dough: A soft mixture of flour, water, and other ingredients, such as salt and sweeteners.

1 Whole grains are received at the cereal factory, inspected, and cleaned. The grains may be used as such or undergo some processing. Often, whole grains are crushed between large metal rollers to remove the outer layer of bran. Then, they are ground more finely into flour.

2 Whole grains or partial grains, such as corn grits, are mixed with water, sweeteners, salt, flavoring agents, vitamins, and minerals in a large pressure cooker. The time, temperature, and speed of rotation vary with the type of grain being cooked.

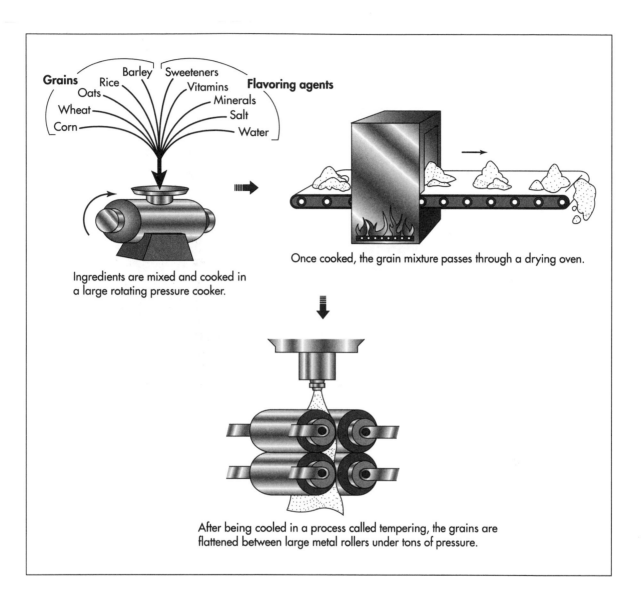

Grains
Barley
Rice
Oats
Wheat
Corn

Sweeteners
Vitamins
Minerals
Salt
Water

Flavoring agents

Ingredients are mixed and cooked in
a large rotating pressure cooker.

Once cooked, the grain mixture passes through a drying oven.

After being cooled in a process called tempering, the grains are
flattened between large metal rollers under tons of pressure.

3 The cooked grains are moved to a conveyor belt, which goes through a drying oven. The cooked grains retain enough water to form a soft, solid mass that can be shaped as needed.

4 If flour is used instead of whole or partial grains, it is cooked in a cooking extruder. This device consists of a long screw inside a heated housing. The movement of the screw mixes the flour with water, flavorings, salt, sweeteners, vitamins, minerals, and sometimes food coloring. The screw moves the flour mixture through the extruder,

fiber: Also called bulk or roughage, it refers to the indigestible part of plant foods.

flour: Finely ground grains.

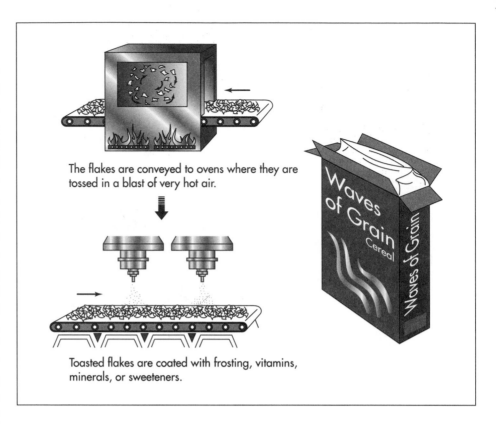

The flakes are conveyed to ovens where they are tossed in a blast of very hot air.

Toasted flakes are coated with frosting, vitamins, minerals, or sweeteners.

grain: The seed or fruit of a cereal grass.

preservative: An ingredient that prevents a food from spoiling.

rancid: Odor or taste of decomposed fats or oils; spoiled.

rolled oats: Oat grains that have had their outer coverings removed, then flattened into flakes with rollers.

shelf life: The length of time a cereal may be stored before it starts losing its freshness.

tempering: The process of allowing cooked grains to sit for several hours in order to even the distribution of moisture.

whole grain/whole wheat grain: A cereal grain with the germ (embryo) and bran (edible seed coat) intact.

yeast: A substance used to help dough rise.

cooking it in the process. The flour comes out of the extruder as a ribbon-like dough. A rotating knife cuts the dough into pellets (small masses), which are then processed the same way as cooked whole or partial grains.

Making flaked cereal

5 The cooked grains are allowed to cool for several hours in order to become tempered, or to allow the moisture content of each grain to get evenly distributed. The tempered grains are then flattened between large metal rollers under tons of pressure, emerging as flakes.

6 The flakes are moved by conveyor belt to ovens in which they are tumbled in a blast of very hot air to remove the remaining moisture. During this process, the flakes are toasted to the desired color and flavor. The dough pellets made from flour (see above) can be made into flakes the same way.

Making puffed cereals

7 Rice grains are usually used to make puffed cereals. The rice grains are cooked, cooled, and dried. As with flaked cereals, the rice grains are passed between metal rollers but are only partially flattened. This process is called bumping.

8 The bumped rice grains are dried again and put into a puffing gun, an oven that holds very hot steam and very high pressure. The oven is quickly opened, reducing the pressure and causing the rice to inflate. The dough pellets from flour can be puffed the same way.

Wheat grains can also be used to make puffed cereals. While the rice grains require no pretreatment, the wheat grains have to have the bran, or outer coat, removed. This may be done in one of two ways. In a process called pearling, the bran is worn off by putting the wheat grain between grindstones. The bran may also be removed by soaking the wheat grains in salt water, which hardens the bran, causing it to break off the grain during puffing.

Making shredded cereals

9 Whole wheat grains are used to make shredded cereals. The wheat grains are boiled in water to let them acquire moisture. The cooked grains are cooled and allowed to temper. Two metal rollers are used for shredding. One roller is smooth, while the other is grooved and has a metal comb. The softened wheat is pushed through the rollers under pressure and shredded in a continuous ribbon by the teeth of the comb. A conveyor belt catches the ribbons, stacking them into layers. The layers are cut into tablets and baked in a very hot oven until the outside is dry and toasted to the desired color. The shredded cereals are put into another oven set at a lower temperature to dry the inside of the cereals. Shredded cereals may also be produced from the dough pellets made of flour.

Making other cereals

10 Cereals can be made from cooked dough into different shapes, such as circles and letters of the alphabet, using a cooking extruder. A mold of the desired shape is attached to the end of the extruder. The ribbon of cooked dough that comes out of the extruder is then cut into smaller pieces by a rotating knife. The shaped pieces are then partially puffed.

The dozens and dozens of types of cereals allow people to choose anything from sugar-coated cereals to healthful bran and whole grain cereals. *Photograph by Kelly A. Quin. Copyright © Kelly A. Quin. Reproduced by permission of the photographer.*

11 Granolas are made by mixing rolled oats and other ingredients, such as brown sugar, nuts, dried fruits, and flavoring agents, and cooking them on a conveyor belt moving through an oven. The cooked mixture is then crumbled to the desired size.

Hot cereals are made by first processing the specific grains—rolling or cutting oats, cracking wheat, or coarsely grinding corn into grits. The grains are partly cooked so that consumers can cook them quickly in hot water. Salt, sweeteners, flavoring agents, and other ingredients may be added to the partly cooked mixture.

Adding coatings

12 After shaping, the cereals may be coated with vitamins, minerals, sweeteners, preservatives, food colors, and flavors, such as fruit juices. A thick, hot syrup may be sprayed on the cereal in a rotating drum. When dry, the syrup forms a white frosting.

Packaging

13 Most cereals are packed in airtight, waterproof plastic bags within cardboard boxes to protect them from spoilage due to moisture. Some cereals, such as shredded wheat, that are not damaged by moisture are placed directly into cardboard boxes or in cardboard boxes lined with plastic. The box tops are sealed with a weak glue to allow for easy opening.

14 The cereals are packaged by an automated machine at a rate of 40 boxes per minute. The completed boxes are packed into cartons that may each hold 12, 24, or 36 boxes. The sealed cartons are then shipped to retailers.

"ENRICHING" AND "FORTIFYING"

Some cereals may lose significant nutrients (vitamins and minerals) during the manufacturing process. For example, the B vitamins are especially likely to be destroyed by heat. After the cooking processes and other heat treatments, the cereals are "enriched" with the nutrients that have been lost. Some cereals may be "fortified," or treated with additional nutrients. Heat-resistant nutrients, such as vitamins A and E, may be cooked into the cereal.

Quality Control

Cleanliness is very important in cereal manufacture. The cereal grains are inspected for any foreign matter when they arrive at the factory and during cooking and shaping. The machines are made of stainless steel, allowing for thorough cleaning and sterilizing with hot steam.

To ensure proper cooking and shaping, workers constantly check the temperature and moisture content of the cereal. Vitamin and mineral contents are measured so that they can be accurately listed in the nutrition information on the packaging. Filled packages are checked for uniform weights.

Stored cereal is tested to determine its shelf life, which is then indicated on the box labels. Testers monitor the freshness of cereal over a certain period of time by subjecting it to temperatures and humidity levels that are higher than normal to speed up spoilage.

The Future

A new development in cereal technology is the twin-screw cooking extruder, in which two screws scrape each other clean as they rotate. This action moves the dough more smoothly through the extruder. Using this extruder along with computers that accurately control temperature and pressure cuts the manufacturing process from 24 hours to less than half an hour.

The cereal industry has responded to the consumers' demand for foods that are more healthful. New cereals in the market include those with added calcium. In the late 1990s, the U.S. Food and Drug Administration (FDA) allowed food manufacturers to put health claims on their product labels, including the benefits of fiber-containing grains and soy protein in lowering the risks of heart disease. Since then, cereals rich in fiber and soy protein have continued to be developed. "Organic" cereals, or cereals made from grains grown without the use of pesticides and/or fertilizers, have also been introduced.

For More Information

Books

Epstein, Rachel. *W.K. Kellogg: Generous Genius.* New York, NY: Grolier Publishing Company, Inc., 2000.

Fast, Robert B., and Elwood F. Caldwell, eds. *Breakfast Cereals and How They Are Made.* 2nd ed. St. Paul, MN: American Association of Cereal Chemists, 2000.

Periodicals

"How Did They Do That?" *Food Insight* (January/February 2001): pp. 2–3.

Web Sites

Adriano, Jackie, and Tamar Genger. "Not Your Mother's Cream of Wheat." *Nutrition Action Health Letter.* http://www.cspinet.org/nah/01_02/index.html (accessed on July 22, 2002).

"Post Heritage." *Kraft Foods.* http://kraftfoods.com/postcereals/heritage_1.html (accessed on July 22, 2002).

"Quaker History." *Quaker Oatmeal.* http://www.quakeroatmeal.com/Archives/History/Indexoat.cfm (accessed on July 22, 2002).

Cigarette

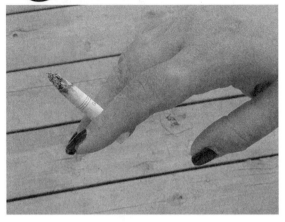

A cigarette consists of shredded tobacco leaves encased in a white, tube-like paper and is used for smoking. About fifteen billion cigarettes are smoked worldwide each day. Americans account for approximately one billion cigarettes smoked every day. More than three million American adolescents under age eighteen smoke half a billion of these cigarettes.

According to the U.S. Surgeon General, about 3,000 American children under age 18 start smoking each day.

A very old habit

More than two thousand years ago, the peoples of Central, North, and South America smoked the dried leaves of the tobacco plant. Different cultures wrapped their tobacco in vegetable leaves or corn husks, or stuffed it into hollow reeds.

In 1492, Christopher Columbus (1451–1506) wrote of receiving dried tobacco leaves as gifts from the natives in the New World. During the 1500s, European explorers brought the tobacco plant back to their native countries.

Early tobacco promoters

In the early 1560s, Jean Nicot de Villemain (1530–1600), the French ambassador to Portugal, touted tobacco as a medicine that could heal many illnesses. People started using tobacco to treat different ailments. Tobacco became very popular among physicians, who even prescribed it

Until 1975 U.S. soldiers were given cigarettes as part of their field rations. *Reproduced by permission of AP/Wide World Photos.*

to patients with breathing difficulties. The tobacco plant was given the name *Nicotiana* after Jean Nicot.

In 1586, Sir Walter Raleigh (1552–1618) of England introduced pipe smoking not to cure illnesses but for pleasure. As a result, many businesses started selling tobacco to the public. It is reported that Sir Raleigh had encouraged Queen Elizabeth I (1533–1603) to try smoking.

Cigarettes' humble beginnings

By 1614, Seville, Spain, had become the world center for cigar production. Beggars in Seville developed the first cigarettes. They collected used cigars and rolled them in paper. However, it took another two hundred years for cigarettes to become popular. In the early 1830s, Egyptian soldiers, for lack of pipes, rolled tobacco in paper. Soon, Turkish soldiers were performing the same rolling of tobacco. During the Crimean War (1853–56), British soldiers picked up the practice from their Turkish and French allies, subsequently popularizing smoking in England.

addiction: A physical and mental dependence on, and craving for, a chemical substance.

aging: A chemical reaction caused by moisture and warm temperature, giving tobacco leaves their distinct taste and aroma.

An American industry

In the American colonies, John Rolfe (1585–1622) of Virginia began the commercial cultivation of tobacco in 1612. Two years later, England imported the first shipment of Virginia-grown tobacco.

In the mid-nineteenth century, cigarettes were introduced in the northern United States. Tobacco merchants in New York City brought in expert cigarette rollers from Europe. Cigarette smoking became popular after the Civil War (1861–65), especially after soldiers from the North passed along some cigarettes to their Southern counterparts. However, cigarettes were expensive because they were rolled by hand, and even a good roller could make only four cigarettes per minute.

The invention of the cigarette-rolling machine in 1880 enabled the mass production of cigarettes and made them affordable to a larger population. The machine patented by James Albert Bonsack (1859–1893) was similar to the machines used today. Although it produced about three cigarettes per second compared to the seventy made by today's faster machines, it nevertheless revolutionized the cigarette industry.

Several developments during the late 1800s benefited the growing cigarette industry. In 1892, the first matchbook matches were patented in the United States. Smokers enjoyed the convenience of carrying a constant supply of matches. During the early 1900s, machines that packaged cigarettes were developed. In 1931, moisture-proof cellophane that preserved the freshness of cigarettes was introduced. Also around that time, an herb called seed flax, commonly grown in the United States, became a source of cigarette paper.

Health hazard

As early as 1892, questions about the consequences of smoking were brought to the attention of the U.S Congress. It took another seven decades for the federal government to limit smoking. By 1963, the average American was smoking over 4,300 cigarettes a year. In 1964, the Surgeon General reported to the nation that cigarette smoking was responsible for the increased deaths in men and the incidence of cancer of the lung and larynx (voice box), as well as chronic bronchitis. The following year, Congress required a warning on all cigarette packages: "Caution: Cigarette smoking may be hazardous to your health."

Raw Materials

The main components (parts) of cigarettes are the leaves from the tobacco plant *Nicotiana*. The tobacco varieties used in cigarette manufacture are

chewing tobacco: Also called spit tobacco, a tobacco product consisting of loose leaves that are held in the mouth and chewed.

curing: The drying of tobacco leaves to remove the natural sap from the leaves.

filter: Also called filter tip, a small tube of porous material attached to the end of a cigarette to catch harmful particles from the smoke.

hogshead: A large, round, wooden barrel in which tobacco leaves are stored for one to three years to develop their flavor and aroma.

nicotine: An addictive substance found in the tobacco plant and in all tobacco products.

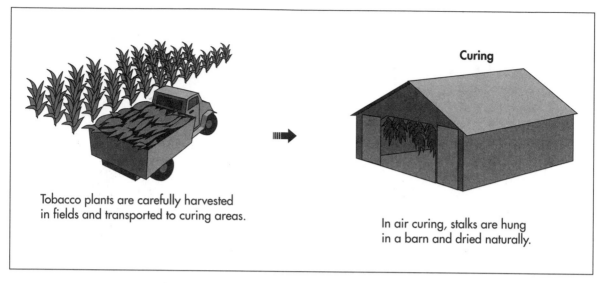

Curing

Tobacco plants are carefully harvested in fields and transported to curing areas.

In air curing, stalks are hung in a barn and dried naturally.

Tobacco grows in two varieties: *Nicotiana tabacum,* or cultivated tobacco, and *Nicotiana rustica,* or wild tobacco. Although transplanting machines are available, the majority of the world's tobacco plants are still planted by hand.

Nicotiana tabacum, or cultivated tobacco, and *Nicotiana rustica,* or wild tobacco. In the United States, Nicotiana tabacum is the only variety cultivated.

Cigarette rolling papers are made of seed flax mixed with paper pulp. These rolling papers are thin and flammable (capable of catching fire). The filters are made of synthetic (artificial) cotton-like fibers that catch particles that are inhaled through the length of the cigarette. The finished cigarettes are packaged in hard or soft cardboard boxes and wrapped in protective cellophane.

The Manufacturing Process

Growing tobacco plants for cigarette manufacture is labor-intensive. This means that tobacco farmers employ a large number of workers from the time the tobacco seeds are planted to the time the leaves are prepared for sale.

Growing the tobacco

1 Tobacco seeds are planted and grown in outdoor frames called seedbeds. In warm areas, the frames are covered with mulch (a mixture of straw, leaves, and similar materials) or a cotton top sheet. In cooler areas, glass or plastic panels are installed for better protection against the cold. Eight to ten weeks later, the seedlings (young plants) that

risk factor: Something that increases a person's chance of developing a disease.

snuff: Powdered tobacco that is sniffed through the nose.

tar: The residue from cigarette smoke.

topping: The process of removing the flowers at the top of the tobacco plant to encourage more leaf growth and larger leaves.

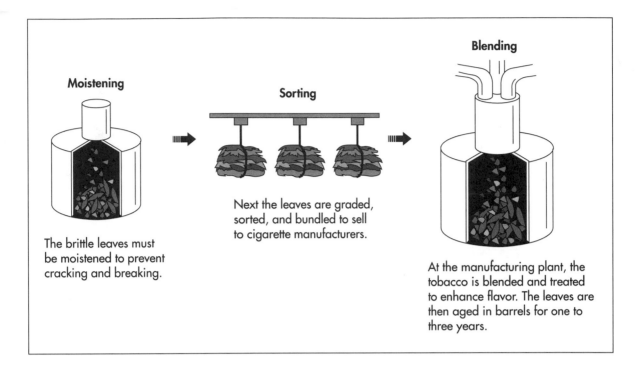

Moistening

The brittle leaves must be moistened to prevent cracking and breaking.

Sorting

Next the leaves are graded, sorted, and bundled to sell to cigarette manufacturers.

Blending

At the manufacturing plant, the tobacco is blended and treated to enhance flavor. The leaves are then aged in barrels for one to three years.

have grown to almost 10 inches (25 centimeters) tall are transplanted to the fields by manual labor.

2 When flowers bloom a few months later, they are removed. The removal of flowers, called topping, results in more leaf growth and larger leaves because leaves get the nutrients that would have gone to the flowers. The tobacco plants are allowed to grow another ninety to one-hundred twenty days before they are harvested.

Harvesting the tobacco

3 Tobacco farmers use one of two methods to harvest the tobacco leaves. In the priming method, the leaves are removed from the plants as they mature and are taken to a curing barn. The remaining leaves are left on the plant to continue to ripen, which may take several weeks. In the stalk-cutting method, the whole plant is cut down, hung from a pole, and allowed to wilt in the field or is transported to the curing barn.

Curing the leaves

4 The harvested leaves are immediately cured, or dried, gradually and carefully in a specially constructed barn. Curing removes all the sap from the leaves, preparing them for further processing.

ventilator: A device used in an enclosed area to circulate air. It can be opened and closed to control the temperature and humidity inside.

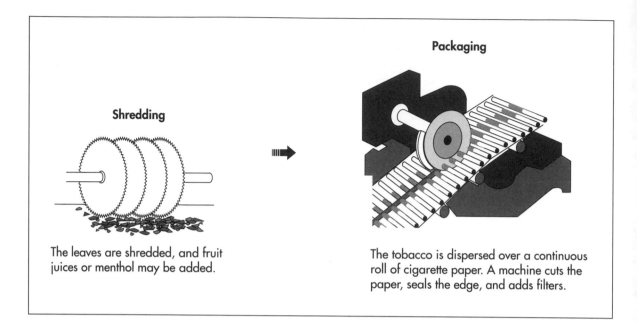

Shredding

The leaves are shredded, and fruit juices or menthol may be added.

Packaging

The tobacco is dispersed over a continuous roll of cigarette paper. A machine cuts the paper, seals the edge, and adds filters.

One of four methods of curing may be used. Air curing is performed in a barn in which the tobacco stalks are hung and allowed to air-dry for four to eight weeks. The curing barn has ventilators, or devices that can be opened and closed to control the temperature and humidity inside. Artificial heat may be used if the weather gets cold or excessively humid.

Flue curing is the fastest method of drying tobacco leaves, taking just four to six days. It is done in small, tightly constructed barns heated by flues, or metal pipes, that are connected to furnaces. In this drying method, smoke does not come in direct contact with the leaves.

Tobacco leaves that are dried by fire curing are first allowed to dry naturally in the curing barn for three to five days. Then the leaves are exposed to the smoke coming from a low-burning wood fire on the barn floor, producing a smoky flavor and aroma. Fire curing takes three to forty days.

Sun curing, as the term implies, consists of drying the leaves in full sunlight.

Moistening and stripping

5 The dried tobacco leaves are conditioned in moistening chambers to prevent breakage when handled. After moistening, the leaves that are attached to the stalk are stripped and sprayed with additional moisture.

Sorting and auctioning

6 The leaves are sorted into grades to indicate their quality. The grading is based, among other things, on leaf size, color, and texture. Then, they are tied in bundles for shipment.

7 The farmers bring the bundled leaves to warehouses, where the bundles are weighed, graded by inspectors of the U.S. Department of Agriculture, and finally auctioned to cigarette manufacturers.

Conditioning, aging, and blending

8 The tobacco leaves that are purchased are transported to the factory, where they are completely air-dried and then conditioned with a uniform amount of moisture. They are packed into large, round, wooden barrels called hogsheads and allowed to age (to undergo a chemical reaction in order to develop a desired flavor and aroma) for one to three years.

9 After the aging process, moisture is again applied to the leaves, and the stems and central veins are removed. Leaves from different types of tobacco are then blended to create the particular flavor desired.

Making the cigarettes

10 The blended leaves are pressed into cakes and shredded by machine. Fruit juices may be added to hold moisture. Flavorings, such as menthol, may also be added. Other flavorings used include sugar, honey, and licorice.

11 To make the cigarettes, a machine distributes the blended tobacco onto a continuous piece of cigarette paper, rolls the paper into a long tube and seals it. The long tube is cut into the desired cigarette lengths. The cigarettes pass through a machine that checks them for the desired length, weight, and circumference. Those that do not meet the requirements are removed. Finally, a device fastens a filter to one end of each cigarette. Modern cigarette machines can produce about seventy cigarettes a second.

Packaging

12 A machine packs the cigarettes twenty to a package. The hard or soft packages are mechanically sealed in cellophane and put into cartons for distribution.

Quality Control

Tobacco farmers ensure the harvest of desirable tobacco leaves by using the strongest seedlings and providing them with the conditions necessary for rapid growth. During the curing process, workers monitor the temperature and humidity inside the curing barn, making sure the leaves dry gradually so that their flavors are preserved. After curing, the right amount of moisture is applied to the leaves to prevent breakage during handling. Care is also taken as the leaves are laid on top of one another in preparation for the aging process.

While the growing of tobacco leaves for cigarette manufacture is labor-intensive, producing the cigarettes is easily done by machine. Quality control involves ensuring products that are uniform in size, weight, and appearance.

WOMEN MARRIED TO A SMOKER HAVE A 91% GREATER RISK OF HEART DISEASE.

Advertisements like this one, stating the negative consequences of smoking, aim to discourage people from picking up the habit. *Reproduced by permission of AP/Wide World Photos.*

The Future

Smoking has been found to be harmful not only to smokers but also to those around them. Studies have shown that cigarette smoke contains about four thousand different chemical compounds, at least forty-three of which are carcinogens (cancer-causing substances). Each year, due to exposure to smoke, an estimated three thousand nonsmoking Americans die of lung cancer. Starting in 1900, medical records showed an increasing number of lung cancer cases. Since the mid-1950s, U.S. Surgeon Generals have publicly opposed smoking as an unnecessary health risk.

Despite the warnings about the danger of smoking, Americans continue to smoke. The U.S. Surgeon General reports that more than three million teens under age eighteen smoke half a billion cigarettes each year. More than one-half claim that they are dependent on cigarettes, meaning that they are addicted to them.

Following medical studies and government reports about the dangers of smoking, manufacturers introduced cigarettes with low tar and nicotine contents. Tar, a residue present in cigarette smoke, contains at least a dozen carcinogens, while nicotine is an addictive substance that is naturally present in tobacco. The government warns that lower levels of tar and nicotine do not necessarily mean the cigarettes are less harmful to health.

In 1998, major cigarette manufacturers agreed to pay almost $206 billion to forty-six states over a number of years for expenses related to the treatment of smoking-related diseases. Although cigarette prices have risen as a result of the monetary settlements, cigarette consumption has not declined much. The government does not foresee cigarette manufacturers closing down their profitable business soon. In fact, U.S. manufacturers have targeted new markets in Asia, Africa, and the former Soviet Union.

For More Information

Books

Connolly, Sean. *Tobacco*. Chicago, IL: Reed Educational & Professional Publishing, 2001.

De Angelis, Gina. *Nicotine & Cigarettes*. Philadelphia, PA: Chelsea House Publishers, 2000.

Parker-Pope, Tara. *Cigarettes: Anatomy of an Industry from Seed to Smoke*. New York, NY: The New Press, 2001.

Periodicals

Shute, Nancy. "Building a Better Butt: Reducing Nicotine in Cigarettes." *U.S. News & World Report*. (September 18, 2000): p. 66.

Squires, Sally. "The Butt Stops Here." *Washington Post*. (February 19, 2002): p. HE01.

Web Sites

Capehart Jr, Thomas C. "Trends in the Cigarette Industry After the Master Settlement Agreement." *U.S. Department of Agriculture Economic Research Service*. http://www.ers.usda.gov/publications/tbs/oct01/tbs250-01/ (accessed on July 22, 2002).

POISON, ANYONE?

Nicotine is a very poisonous chemical that is used in many insecticides (chemical substances used to kill insects). Compared to insecticides, cigarettes contain a small amount of nicotine, which is the reason it does not cause instant death. However, nicotine is addictive so that smokers become physically and mentally dependent on cigarettes. The more cigarettes a person smokes, the more poisonous chemicals he or she ingests, including tar, carbon monoxide, and hydrogen cyanide. Other tobacco products, including cigars and smokeless tobacco (chewing or spit tobacco, or snuff), also contain nicotine.

"The Surgeon General's Report for Kids about Smoking." *Centers for Disease Control and Prevention.* http://www.cdc.gov/tobacco/sgr/sgr4kids/sgrmenu.htm (accessed on July 22, 2002).

Cotton Candy

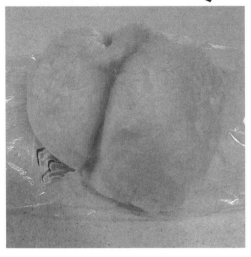

Photograph by Kelly A. Quin. Copyright © Kelly A. Quin. Reproduced by permission of the photographer.

C otton candy is a light and fluffy sugar candy, which resembles cotton wool. It is made by heating sugar to a very high temperature and then spinning the melted sugar to produce fine sugar threads. Cotton candy has a fibrous texture that makes it unique from other sugar candies. The fibrous threads have many of the same characteristics as cotton fibers, which is how cotton candy got its name.

Cotton candy is a popular food at amusement parks and carnivals and is typically sold individually as a large mass wrapped around a cardboard cone. When the threads are collected on a cone, they are packed loosely so that a certain amount of air gets trapped between the fibers. This increases the volume of the candy, giving it a light and fluffy texture. Cotton candy remains a favorite among people of all ages. Today, it is also sold in malls, video shops, movie theaters, toy stores, grocery stores, and sports arenas.

A typical cotton candy cone contains about one hundred calories.

Sweet history

Sugar, the main ingredient in cotton candy, was not known during ancient times. Many early cultures made candies using honey mixed with such ingredients as fruit, nuts, and spices. Other sweeteners used included date syrup, fig syrup, and sugar cane juice. The ancient Hindus and Chinese grew sugar cane and extracted the juice for sweetening. There is evidence that when Persia (now called Iran) invaded India during the early 500s B.C.E., the conquerors found what they described as plants that pro-

Cotton candy has always been an extremely popular snack at local fairs and amusement parks. *Reproduced by permission of Hulton Archive.*

automated machine: A machine that operates and regulates itself without human intervention.

cellophane: A thin, transparent material made from wood pulp used as a moisture-proof wrapper.

color additive: Any dye or substance that gives color when added to a food.

duced honey without bees. In later years, Persia cultivated sugar cane and refined it to produce cane sugar, some of which was used to make candy.

The Arabic people who invaded Persia during the seventh century discovered sugar cane, which subsequently was introduced to Spain, North Africa, and Sicily in Italy. Sugar cane did not reach England until the eleventh century, and even then, it was scarce. Some of it was made into candy, which for many years was a luxury item available only to the wealthy.

In 1747, German scientist Andreas Marggraf (1707–1782) discovered sugar in beet juice. Fifty years later, in 1798, his student Franz Achard (1753–1821) produced the first beet sugar. These accomplishments and the invention of candy-making machinery contributed to the growth of the candy industry in Europe during the eighteenth and nineteenth centuries.

Fairy floss

In the United States, the invention of candy-making machines also contributed to the growth of the candy industry. These machines were semiautomatic and allowed production on a large scale. In 1897, William J. Morrison (1860–1926) and John C. Wharton, candymakers from Nashville, Tennessee, invented the first electric machine for making cotton candy. The machine consisted of a spinning bowl with tiny holes. Sugar that was heated in the bowl melted and was forced through the tiny holes, forming fine strands of sugar. They called the feathery candy "Fairy Floss" and first introduced it to the world at the St. Louis World's Fair (Missouri) in 1904.

The portable machine soon became very popular. Operators could transport the machine to circuses, carnivals, and ball parks and sell individual servings of the candy. At some point, the name became cotton candy. Mass production of cotton candy occurred after 1972 when an automatic manufacturing machine was invented.

Raw Materials

Sugar is the main ingredient used in the manufacture of cotton candy. Its chemical name is sucrose, and it is obtained primarily from sugar cane and sugar beet. Sucrose is commonly called cane sugar. In cotton candy, sugar is responsible for the candy's physical structure, as well as its taste and mouthfeel (physical sensation of food in the mouth).

Other ingredients are needed to produce the popular characteristics of cotton candy. Color additives, or dyes, are added to white sugar to produce the different colors that make cotton candy appealing to the eye. The U.S. Food and Drug Administration (FDA) regulates the use of color additives in food. Cotton candy can be made to be almost any color by combining FDA-approved color additives, including Red Dye #40 (commonly called allura Red AC), Yellow Dye #5 (tartrazine), Yellow Dye #6 (sunset yellow), and Blue Dye #1 (brilliant blue FCF). In addition to the standard pink and blue colors, cotton candy can be found in other colors, such as purple, red, yellow, and brown.

Along with color, natural and artificial flavors are added to give the sugary treat extra appeal. Cotton candy is available in a variety of flavors, including bubble gum, chocolate, banana, raspberry, watermelon, cherry, mint, vanilla, grape, cherry, and piña colada (pineapple and coconut).

mouthfeel: Physical sensation of food in the mouth.

semiautomatic machine: A machine that partly operates itself and partly needs a person to run it.

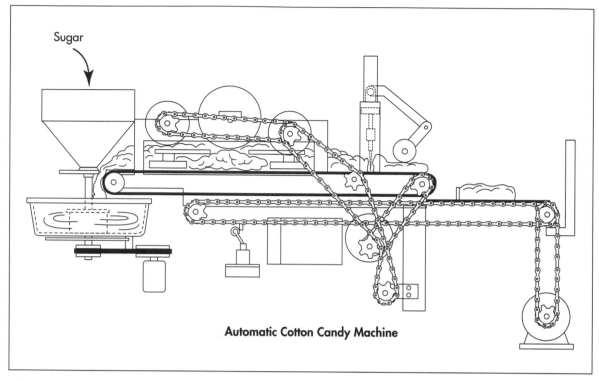

Sugar

Automatic Cotton Candy Machine

After processing the sugar granules into extruded sugar strands, the strands of cotton candy are pulled onto a conveyor belt and transferred into a sizing container.

Different packaging materials are used in cotton candy manufacture. Clear, cellophane bags are typically used because they are moisture-proof. Moisture can make cotton candy rubbery and sticky.

The Manufacturing Process

Two types of machines are used to produce cotton candy. One machine is semiautomatic and is used to make single servings that are sold at carnivals and amusement parks. The other is a fully automated machine that produces large volumes of cotton candy for widespread distribution. Both machines are similar and are discussed below.

Sugar processing

1 Powdered sugar is put into a large, circular, stainless steel hopper (a bin). Color additives and flavors are then added to the sugar, and the three ingredients are mixed. The hopper is fitted with a tapered

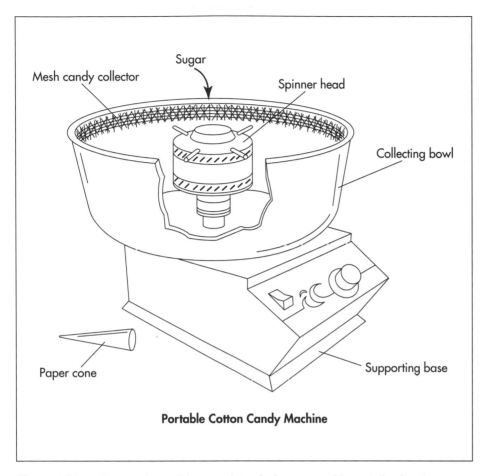

Portable Cotton Candy Machine

Sugar

Mesh candy collector

Spinner head

Collecting bowl

Paper cone

Supporting base

The portable cotton candy machine consists of a large pan with a rotating heating core in the middle. Operators make individual servings at popular venues such as the circus, carnival, and ball park.

bottom that feeds the sugar mixture into an extruder. The extruder is a spinning metal cylinder with a heating element and holes along its sides. Manufacturers may also use a ready-mixed sugar mixture called floss sugar, which comes in a variety of colors and flavors.

2 Inside the extruder, the sugar is heated, melting into a very hot liquid. The extruder spins, forcing the liquid sugar through the holes in its side. As the sugar leaves the extruder, it encounters air and cools, forming a delicate web of very fine threads. The threads are collected in a large circular pan surrounding the extruder. To prevent the threads from thickening into a semisolid mass, the workers make sure little, or no, moisture is present.

Cotton candy vendors often set up their stands on boardwalks where people walking by can buy the treat.
Reproduced by permission of Corbis Corporation.

Candy collection

3 If the machine produces a small amount of cotton candy, such as machines found at fairs or malls, the machine operator collects the threads of cotton candy. The operator takes a cardboard cone and passes it around the sides of the circular pan. As the cardboard cone is passed around, the sugar fibers stick to it, forming a fluffy mass. It is immediately sold to the consumer.

Cotton candy produced in large quantities undergoes a different collection process. After exiting the automated machine, the cotton candy threads are pulled onto a conveyor belt and transferred into a sizing container. Here, the cotton candy threads are combined into a continuous bundle.

4 In the sizing container, the bundle of cotton candy is formed into a consistent shape. Devices called rollers are positioned on the top and sides of the conveyor belt to perform the shaping with a minimum of force so as not to change the texture or characteristics of the cotton candy. The rollers are typically coated with a nonstick substance, such

as Teflon®. As the candy leaves the sizing container, it has the shape of a continuous block with a fixed height and width.

Cutting

5 After the shaping process, the cotton candy is transported by conveyor belt to a knife blade. The knife is mounted above the conveyor belt and slides down to cut the cotton candy into segments of a specific length. The knife is drawn back, and the cotton candy moves to another area where another roller maintains its shape.

Packaging

6 The completed cotton candy is transferred to a packaging machine. It is automatically put into a cellophane bag or other type of packaging and sealed. Moisture-proof packaging is used to prevent spoilage, as well as changes that moisture may bring on, such as causing the candy to get sticky. The sealed bags are passed under a coding device where they are marked with information, such as batch number and date of production. The bags are carefully put into boxes. The boxes are stacked on wooden pallets, transferred to trucks, and shipped to the local supermarkets. The entire process from loading the sugar into the cotton candy machine to putting the finished candy into boxes takes only a few minutes.

Quality Control

Quality control begins with checking the incoming ingredients. The ingredients are tested in a laboratory to make sure they meet specifications. Tests include analyzing an ingredient's physical properties, such as particle size, appearance, color, and flavor. Certain chemical properties of the ingredients may also be evaluated. Manufacturers generally have their own tests to ensure that the ingredients will produce a consistent, quality batch of cotton candy.

The packaging is also inspected. The odor check is an important quality control, because bags that have acquired off-odors during processing may pass on these undesirable odors to the cotton candy. The packaging is also checked for its moisture-vapor transmission rate. Other properties checked are the grease resistance and physical appearance of the packaging. Cotton candy that is manufactured properly, using quality ingredients and packaging, will remain fresh for about six months.

Manufacturers also monitor the characteristics of the finished products. As with the raw ingredients, the finished cotton candies are tested for their appearance, texture, color, and flavor. A newly prepared batch may be monitored by comparing its characteristics against established standards. A panel of specially trained personnel also performs sensory tests of taste, texture, and odor. Finally, standard industry instrument tests that measure certain product properties may also be done.

The Future

The basic cotton candy has not changed much since it was first introduced. However, as the popularity of cotton candy continues, manufacturers experiment with new flavors and colors.

Most of the improvements in the manufacture of cotton candy have to do with improving the design of machines in order to make more candies. For example, some machines have bigger hoppers for holding more powdered sugar. It is expected that future improvements will involve computer-controlled machines that will produce cotton candy more efficiently, economically, and safely.

For More Information

Books

Alikonis, Justin J. *Candy Technology.* Westport, CT: AVI Publishing Company, Inc., 1979.

Web Sites

"Food Color Facts." *U.S. Food and Drug Administration.* http://www.cfsan.fda.gov./~lrd/colorfac.html (accessed on July 22, 2002).

"Sugar Facts: Growing and Processing Sugar." *The Sugar Association.* http://www.sugar.org/facts/grow.html (accessed on July 22, 2002).

DVD Player

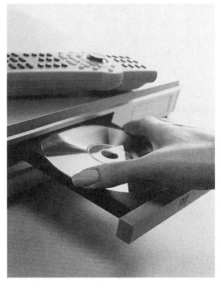

A digital video disk or digital versatile disk (DVD) is an optical (using light) storage medium with digital data, or information that has been translated into a number code. A laser (a narrow, intense beam of light) is used to store the digital information on a DVD in the form of indentations called pits (holes) and lands (surfaces between the pits).

The indentations are laid out on a continuous spiral track, which starts near the center of the disk, circling around the whole disk in a structure similar to that found on vinyl records. Laser is again used in recovering the stored information on the DVD. Using a laser beam, the DVD player "reads" the indentations, reproducing the movie, music, or data stored in the disk.

A DVD is the same size and thickness as a CD, but it can hold at least seven times more data.

The idea of storing information in a device and then reproducing that information goes back to the early nineteenth century. In 1801, French silk weaver Joseph-Marie Jacquard (1752–1834) invented a series of punched metal cards to store information for weaving patterns. Jacquard's loom, controlled by the information stored in the punch cards, made complicated patterns automatically. In fact, the idea behind Jacquard's invention was initially responsible for the idea of storing programs for computers.

History

The development of DVD players began with the introduction of the first audio (sound) CDs (compact disks) and CD players in the early 1980s. Video

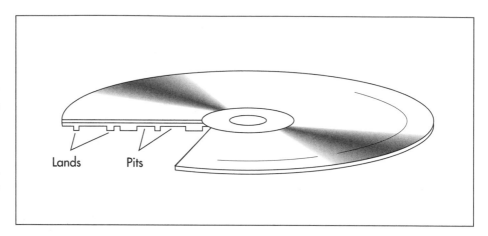

A DVD contains a series of indentations called "pits" and "lands." Using a laser beam, a DVD player reads these indentations, converts the reflected light into electrical signals, and recreates the movie, music, or data stored on the disk.

Lands   Pits

compact disk (CD): Like the DVD, the CD is an optical storage medium with digital information. CDs typically store recorded music.

digital: Pertaining to information that has been translated into a number code.

laser: Stands for Light Amplification by Simulated Emission of Radiation. It can refer to the device that produces the light beam or the light beam itself. Unlike ordinary light, which consists of different colors and spreads out in many directions, laser is a single intense color that stays focused in one direction.

microchip: A small piece of semiconductor material, such as silicon, that carries electronically connected parts.

optical: Pertaining to or using light.

(visual) CD players were introduced later in the decade, although they never became popular enough to replace videocassette recorders (VCRs).

As other advancements in CD technology were occurring, including computer CDs and recordable CD players, researchers continued to search for ways to improve the storage capacity of CDs. Then, scientists discovered that they could use a red laser to place more pits on the surface of the disk. (Laser light, unlike ordinary light that spreads out in all directions, is tightly focused and intense.) This led to the creation of the DVD. In 1997, the first DVD players were introduced.

Packing it in

The DVD was developed as an improved form of CD technology. The same size (4.75 inches, or 12 centimeters, in diameter) and thickness (1.2 millimeters) as the CD, the DVD can hold at least seven times more data. A DVD can store much more information than a CD because the pits are smaller than those on a CD; therefore, more pits can fit on a track. Also, the tracks are arranged closer together, allowing for more tracks on the disk. Scientists observe that if the whole spiral track could be taken off a single-sided, single-layer DVD disk and placed in a straight line, it would measure over seven miles long.

DVDs vary in the amount of storage space, depending upon their physical structures. In terms of movies, the amount of viewing time can range from about two hours for a single-sided, single-layer disk to eight hours for a double-sided, double-layer disk. In comparison, a CD stores about seventy-five minutes of music. No matter how many layers are in the DVD disk, the thickness remains the same.

Although the disk is capable of storing a large amount of data, it cannot hold all the information of a full-length movie. In order to fit the movie on a disk, the moviemaker uses a compression method to reduce the amount of data stored. Each second of a movie consists of about thirty still (nonmoving) images called frames. When played in fast motion, the frames are translated by the human brain and seen by the human eye as one movement. Therefore, a movie calls for a huge number of still frames. During the process of compression, a frame that is similar to a previous frame is removed, thus allowing more room for storage.

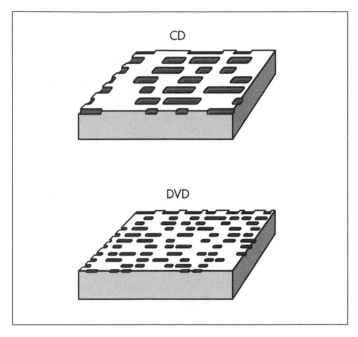

Although the CD and DVD have the same size and thickness, the DVD can store more information because of pits that are smaller in size and tracks that are more closely arranged.

A versatile machine

The DVD player is quite versatile (having varied functions). It is backwards-compatible, which means that the machine can play CD music. In contrast, a CD player cannot play DVD music. DVD players that hold more than one disk are called changers. A jukebox-type player can store up to two hundred disks to house an entire music or movie collection.

The player is so powerful it can read the second layer of stored data of a single-sided disk through the first layer, so that there is no need to flip the disk over. Starting at the center of the disk, the laser reads the first layer of pits and lands, continuously moving outward. When the laser reaches the end of the spiral track at the outermost part of the disk, the player quickly refocuses the laser beam on the second layer. Without missing a beat, the player reads the disk, staying at the outer part of the disk, but proceeding in the opposite direction. There is no interruption in the movie sequence because the data on the second layer has been recorded backwards.

photodiode: Also called a photosensor; a light-sensitive device that changes a light code into electrical signals.

pits and lands: Microscopic indentations on a DVD that store the information used to recreate a movie.

semiconductor: A nonmetallic material that conducts electricity.

DVD players are more frequently being found in homes next to, and sometimes in place of, VCRs. *Photograph by Kelly A. Quin. Copyright © Kelly A. Quin. Reproduced by permission of the photographer.*

The player also has the ability to decompress the data stored on a DVD. It rebuilds the whole movie as the viewer is watching it, filling in the missing information that had been eliminated during the compression process (see above).

DVD players that reproduce movies

videocassette recorder (VCR): A device that records and plays back television programs and movies by means of a videotape contained in a rectangular plastic case.

DVD data can come in the form of video, audio, or computer information. The following explanation will focus on DVD players that hook up to a television set for watching movies. A typical single-sided, single-layer DVD disk contains about two hours of movie.

DVD players reproduce home movies that are comparable to cinema movies in picture quality and sound. Since no part of the DVD player touches the disk when the movie is playing, the picture and sound quality of the movie remains the same as the first time it was played. Compare this to a video tape that loses some of its original picture and sound quality every time it is played.

A DVD player lets the viewer access standard DVD features, including different languages (up to eight languages), various subtitles (up to thirty-two languages), behind-the-scenes footage, and a wide-screen image, even when viewed on a standard television screen. Other features include uncut versions of the film, closed-captioned viewing (text of the audio information) for the hearing-impaired, and parental locks, by which an adult could set the machine to play the PG-rated version of an R-rated movie. The DVD video may also include commentary tracks, in which an individual connected to the movie talks about it as the film unfolds. Then, there are hidden surprises, such as previews of other movies.

Design

DVD players are designed like CD players. The simple exterior is made of plastic, with a front panel of plastic buttons. Some players

The sale and rental of DVD movies has skyrocketed and movie rental places continue to expand their collection of DVD titles. *Reproduced by permission of AP/Wide World Photos.*

have a plastic tray that comes out of the machine to accept disks. Others have an automatic feed system into which the disk is inserted.

Like a CD player, a DVD player has three main components—a disk drive mechanism, an optical assembly system, and an internal electronic circuit board. The disk drive mechanism typically consists of a spindle that holds the disk and a motor that spins it. The optical system assembly includes the laser, the photodiode (also called a photosensor), lenses, and mirrors. The circuit board contains all the electronic pieces for converting the data into the original movie recorded on the DVD disk.

How does it work?

When a disk is inserted into a DVD player, the player spins it and focuses a laser beam on the spiral track containing the pits and lands. The lens and prism (mirror) help focus the laser beam properly. As the laser

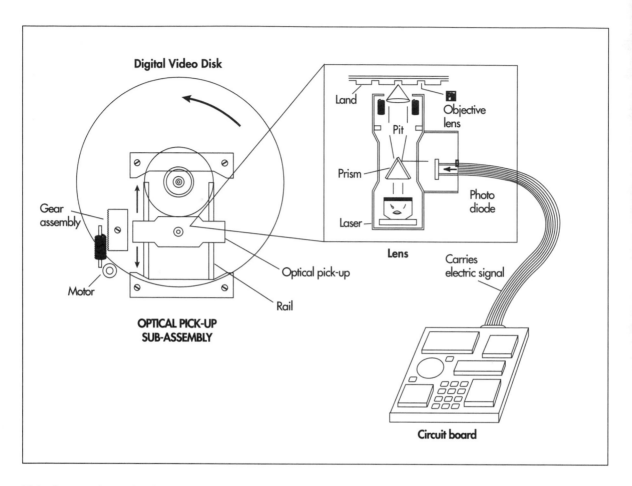

Digital Video Disk

Land

Pit

Objective lens

Prism

Photo diode

Laser

Lens

Gear assembly

Motor

Optical pick-up

Rail

OPTICAL PICK-UP SUB-ASSEMBLY

Carries electric signal

Circuit board

This diagram shows the three parts of a DVD player—the disk drive mechanism, the optical system assembly, and the electronic circuit board—and how they work together to reproduce the movie stored on the disk. As the spindle holds the disk, the motor spins it. The optical system assembly reads the pits and lands on the underside of the disk and converts the reflected light into electrical signals. The signals that are passed on to the electronic circuit board are in turn converted into the data stored on the DVD disk.

hits the pits and lands, light of varying intensity is reflected back by the disk. The photodiode, which is light-sensitive, reads the variations in light intensity and converts them into electrical signals. The signals are passed on to the electronic circuit board, which in turn recreates the movie.

A portable movie theater

DVD players can come as portable units that look like laptop computers. They not only play movies, but also CDs. They are lightweight and have a rechargeable battery pack. The screen is typically about seven inches, although the smallest player has a 5.8-inch screen. As with regular-sized machines, portable units play movies and music of excellent quality.

Raw Materials

The DVD player and disk are made out of a variety of materials. Some are familiar materials such as glass and plastic, while others are less known.

DVD player materials

The cabinet that houses the different components of the DVD player is made of aluminum. The laser device consists of a glass tube filled with gas, as well as a small power supply to produce the laser beam. The photodiode and the main components on the circuit board are typically made of silicon. Silicon is a nonmetallic material that can conduct electricity. Its unique ability to act as an off–on switch makes it a valuable component of electronic equipment.

Disk materials

Polycarbonate plastic, the same material used in making bulletproof windows, makes up the base material of the disk. The plastic is coated with a thin layer of metal, such as aluminum, silver, or gold, for reflecting the laser light. It is on the metal that the pits and lands are recorded. The surface of the disk is further coated with a hard layer of lacquer to protect it from damage. Finally, a label is applied over the disk.

The Manufacturing Process

The components of a DVD player are made by separate companies and then put together by the manufacturer. The main components include the optical system assembly, disk drive mechanism, and internal electronic circuit board.

Optical system assembly

1 The optical assembly system is made up of a laser, photodiode, prism, and lenses. The laser and photodiode are placed on a plastic housing, and the other components are placed in specific places.

SLEEK AND SLIM

A new addition to the family of DVD players is a space-saver measuring 10 inches (252 mm) by 7.25 inches (184 mm) by 2.4 inches (61 mm). Unlike the traditional desktop players, Sony's DVD Style Cube can be positioned and operated in three ways—vertically, horizontally, or mounted to the wall. It comes in silver or black, has a slot-loading disk mechanism, and is intended for use in any room in the house.

Many cars and vans now come equipped with DVD players inside so passengers can watch movies to entertain themselves on long drives. *Reproduced by permission of AP/Wide World Photos.*

Each piece has to be arranged just right, or the system will not perform properly. Electrical connections are put in place, and the optical system is ready to be attached to the disk drive mechanism.

Disk drive mechanism

2 The optical system assembly is connected to the motor that will drive it. The motor is then connected to the other parts of the disk drive, including the loading tray (if present) and the spindle motor. After other gear and belts are attached, the entire assembly is placed in the main body.

Internal electronic circuit board

3 The process of putting the circuit board together is done in a clean room kept free of nearly all dust particles that can damage the board. A printed board showing how the different electronic components should be arranged is passed through a series of machines. Electronic pieces, including

microchips that direct the electronic processes of the machine, are plugged into the board. Then the board with the electronic pieces on it is washed to further clean it in preparation for soldering.

4 Soldering is the process by which the electronic pieces are permanently attached to the board. This is done by passing the bottom of the board through solder (a mixture of metals) that has been melted, filling the appropriate spots that would hold the components in place. As the board is allowed to cool, the solder hardens, holding the pieces in place.

Final assembly

5 When all the components are ready, the electronic board is hooked to the rest of the machine, and the main cover is attached. The finished DVD players are sent to a packaging station where they are boxed along with accessories, such as disks, manuals, and power cords.

Quality Control

To ensure the quality of the DVD players, visual and electrical inspections are done throughout the entire production process. Defects that are found are corrected. In addition, each machine is played to see if it performs as expected. The testing is done under different conditions, such as excessive heat and humidity.

The Future

Even though DVD technology is relatively new, DVD players are expected to replace both VCRs and CD players in the early twentieth century. Researchers continue to look for ways to fit more data on the DVD disk. An area of research includes new laser technologies involving more powerful lasers to both write and read the data that make up a movie. Blue laser, narrower and brighter than the red laser, could help store more data on a disk. In the meantime, almost every recent movie has been made available on DVD. In addition, old movies are being converted to DVD form.

Manufacturers continue to improve on the standard DVD player. For those consumers who want the option of a VCR, some manufacturers have combined a DVD player with a VCR to form one unit. A person can watch a DVD movie and tape a television program onto the VCR tape at the same time. Experts foresee the combination of DVD and Internet technologies, in which the high-quality video and audio content of a DVD would be combined with the ever-changing information from the Internet.

For More Information

Books

Morgan, Nina. *Lasers*. Austin, TX: Steck-Vaughn Company, 1997.

Ross, John. *DVD Player Fundamentals*. Indianapolis, IN: Sams Technical Publishing, 2000.

Periodicals

"The Disc That Saved Hollywood: Jealous execs… Backroom deals… The inside story of how DVDs became the entertainment industry's most lucrative product." *Newsweek*. (August 20, 2001): pp. 30-33.

"DVD Players." *Consumer Reports*. (December 2001): pp. 30-33.

Poor, Alfred. "CDs and DVDs." *PC Magazine*. (May 4, 1999): pp. 207-209.

Escalator

An escalator is a moving stairway that transports passengers up and down the floors of a building. It is generally constructed in areas where elevators would be impractical. These areas include shopping malls, airports, transit systems, trade centers, hotels, and public buildings.

Photograph by Kelly A. Quin. Copyright © Kelly A. Quin. Reproduced by permission of the photographer.

It is estimated that there are at least 33,000 escalators in the United States. About ninety billion people ride escalators each year. Escalators and their cousins, moving walkways, move at approximately 1 to 2 feet (0.3 to 0.6 meter) per second. The maximum angle of inclination (slope) is 30 degrees with a standard rise of about 60 feet (18 meters).

It is estimated that about ninety billion people ride escalators each year.

An escalator is a very clever invention. Escalators can be built in the same physical space that stairs would occupy, and yet they have the capacity to move larger numbers of people. Except during periods of heavy traffic, there is generally no waiting time to get on an escalator. They can be used to guide people toward main exits or special exhibits. Escalators can also be constructed outdoors and provided with the proper covering in case of bad weather.

Escalator inventors

In 1891, American engineer Jesse W. Reno (1861–1947) patented the first escalator, which he originally envisioned when he was sixteen years old. Described by Reno as "a new and useful endless conveyor," the first escalator was constructed at Coney Island in Brooklyn, New York, as an amusement ride. Passengers rode on supports attached to a conveyor belt at an incline of about 25 degrees.

The invention of the escalator as we know it today is credited to Charles D. Seeberger, who had bought Reno's patent and added horizontal steps in the late 1890s. Seeberger coined the word escalator by combining elevator and *scala,* the Latin word for steps. Seeberger and his employer, Otis Elevator Company, installed the first step-type escalator for public use at the Paris Exhibition of 1900, where it won first prize. In 1910, Seeberger sold his patents to the company. In 1921, Otis Elevator Company manufactured a machine that was the forerunner of today's escalator.

Components

Although numerous improvements have been made to the original escalator, the basic design remains in use today. It consists of stationary (nonmoving) top and bottom landing platforms, a metal truss that connects the two platforms, two pairs of tracks on which a collapsible staircase is pulled by a continuous chain that loops around two pairs of gears (toothed wheels), and handrails that move with the staircase.

Top and bottom landing platforms

The top and bottom landing platforms house the curved sections of the tracks. The top platform contains the motor, which turns the two drive gears, which in turn move the two continuous chain loops on each side of the movable staircase. The bottom platform holds the return gears (also called the return wheels). The two platforms also hold the ends of the truss in place.

Each of the platforms also contains a floor plate and a comb plate. The floor plate is the area where the passengers stand before boarding the moving staircase. This plate is flush with the floor. It is either removable or hinged (fitted with a joint that fastens it to the floor) to allow easy access to the machinery below, if necessary. The comb plate is the piece between the floor plate and the moving staircase. It is so named because its edge has a series of grooves resembling the teeth of a comb. The grooves of the comb plate mesh with the matching grooves found on the edges of the steps. This design makes the gap between the stair and the landing platforms very small, preventing objects from getting caught in the gap.

The truss

The truss is the hollow metal structure that extends between the lower and upper landing platforms and supports the escalator. It consists of two

die-cast: Shaped in a mold by pressure.

patent: To obtain from the government the sole right to make and sell an invention for a certain period of time.

tensile strength: The maximum stretching force that a material can bear before it breaks.

truss: The metal structure that extends between the lower and upper landing platforms and supports the escalator.

The escalator steps function in a unique way, changing from an erect staircase to a collapsible staircase as needed. The tracks are the farthest from each other along the straight section of the truss. This causes the back of one step to be at a 90-degree angle in relation to the step behind it. This right angle bends the steps into a stair shape. At the top and bottom of the escalator, the two tracks meet so that the front and back wheels of the steps are almost in a straight line. This causes the steps to collapse or flatten on each other by fitting into each other's grooved edges, and they easily travel around the bend in the curved section of the track. The tracks carry the steps down along the underside of the truss until they reach the bottom landing, where they pass through another curved section of the track before exiting the bottom landing. At this point, the tracks separate and the steps once again assume a staircase arrangement. The cycle is repeated continuously as the steps are pulled from bottom to top and back to bottom again.

side sections joined together with cross braces across the bottom and just below the top. The ends of the truss are attached to the landing platforms using steel or concrete supports. The truss also supports two handrails, which are coordinated to move at the same speed as the staircase.

The track system

The track system is built into the truss to guide the step chains, which continuously pull the steps from the bottom platform to the top in a continuous loop. The track system consists of two tracks, or rails—the step-wheel track (inner rail) for the front wheels of the steps and the trailer-wheel track (outer rail) for the back wheels of the steps. The position of the tracks with respect to each other causes the steps to form a staircase as they move out from under the comb plate.

The steps

The steps are solid, one-piece, die-cast aluminum (aluminum shaped in a mold using pressure). Rubber mats may be attached to the step surfaces to reduce slippage, and yellow border lines may be added to clearly indicate the edges of the steps. The two long edges of each step have grooves that fit the comb plates of the top and bottom landing platforms.

Each step has an axle that is connected to the axles of the other steps by a continuous metal chain that forms a loop. Each step has four wheels that run on two separate tracks on each side of the staircase. The step wheels (front wheels) are pulled by the drive gear at the top landing platform, while the trailer wheels (back wheels) simply "trail" after the front wheels.

The handrails

An escalator has a handrail on each side. The handrails move at the same speed as the steps and serve as supports. Each handrail is a moving belt that is pulled along its track by a chain, which is connected to the drive gear by a series of pulleys.

The handrail is made up of four sections. At the center is a "slider," a layer of cotton or synthetic (artificial) fabric, which allows the handrail to move smoothly along its track. The next layer, known as the tension member, consists of either steel cable or flat steel tape. It provides the handrail with the necessary tensile strength (stretch) and flexibility. On top of the tension member is chemically treated rubber that helps prevent the layers from separating. Finally, the cover is a blend of synthetic plastic and rubber, designed to resist the wear and tear of daily use.

The three inner layers of fabric, steel, and rubber are shaped by skilled workers before being subjected to pressure from machines called presses, which fuse them together. The cover is made by feeding rubber through a computer-controlled extrusion machine, which forces the rubber through a mold to form a continuously shaped piece.

Design

Aside from determining the escalator's style and colors (handrails and side panels), the architects and designers have to consider several factors.

Physical factors

Physical factors, such as the vertical and horizontal distances to be covered by the escalator, are very important because they will determine the pitch (angle of slope) and the actual height of the escalator. In addition, the building structure has to be able to support the heavy components (parts) of the escalator.

The escalator should be situated where the general public can easily find it and get on it with ease. It should not be in a tight spot or lead to confined spaces. Traffic patterns must also be anticipated. In some buildings, escalators are used simply for moving people from one floor to another. In other cases, escalators are built for specific purposes, such as to funnel people toward a main exit or exhibit.

The use of escalators not only allows malls to have more levels but also helps to control the heavy flow of people that would be too much for the slower elevators. *Reproduced by permission of AP/Wide World Photos.*

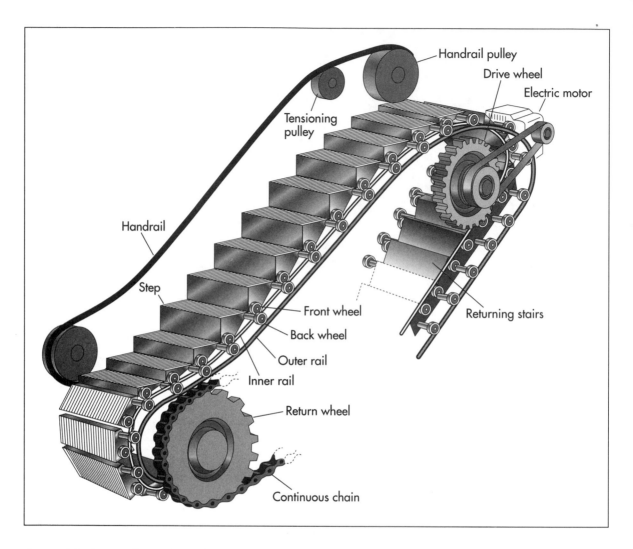

An escalator is a continuously moving staircase. Each stair has a pair of wheels on each side, one at the front and the other at the rear. The wheels run on two rails. At the top and bottom of the escalator, the inner rail dips beneath the outer rail so that the bottom of the stair flattens, making it easier for riders to get on and off.

Carrying capacity

The carrying capacity of the escalator is an important aspect of its design. An escalator is designed to carry a certain maximum number of people, depending on its design. For example, a single-width escalator traveling at about 1.5 feet (0.45 meter) per second can move approximately 170 people per five-minute period. On the other hand, wider models traveling at up to 2 feet (0.6 meter) per second can move more than two and one-half times that number, or about 450 people, in the same time period. In addition, the carrying capacity must be able to accommodate peak periods, during which the most passengers board the escalator. For example, escalators at train stations must be able to handle the increased flow of people discharged from a train without causing back-ups at the escalator entrance.

Safety

Safety is a major consideration in escalator design. The floor opening may be protected against fire by the addition of automatic sprinklers or fireproof shutters. The escalator may also be situated in an enclosed fire-protected hall. To prevent overheating of the motor and gears, proper ventilation should be provided.

If the escalator is the primary means of transportation between floors, a traditional staircase can be located near it. An elevator near an escalator is also ideal for accommodating wheelchairs and people with disabilities.

The Manufacturing Process

Two types of companies supply escalators. Primary manufacturers build the equipment, while secondary suppliers design and install the equipment. In most cases, the secondary suppliers receive the equipment from the manufacturer and make the necessary changes.

1 The first stage of escalator construction is to establish the design, as described above. The manufacturer uses this design information to construct the customized equipment. The tracks, step chains, stair assembly, and motorized gears and pulleys are all bolted into place on the truss. The handrails are carefully coiled (wound into a loop) and packed. All the equipment is then shipped to the supplier.

2 Before installation, the top and bottom landing areas are prepared for connection to the escalator. Concrete fittings are poured, and the steel framework that will hold the truss in place is attached.

3 After the escalator arrives at the site, it is jockeyed into position between the top and bottom landing holes. Several methods are used to lift the truss into place. One method uses a scissors-lift apparatus mounted on a wheeled support platform. The scissors lift is outfitted with a locator assembly to help in vertical and angular alignment of the escalator. The upper end of the truss is first aligned with the support wall at the upper landing and then placed on this support wall. The lower

The risers of an escalator separate into moving stairs but can also be a hazard for objects, such as shoelaces, to get caught in. *Photograph by Kelly A. Quin. Copyright © Kelly A. Quin. Reproduced by permission of the photographer.*

end of the truss is put into a pit on the floor of the lower landing. If the handrails come separately, they are connected to the appropriate chains after the escalator is installed.

4 The escalator is connected to the power source, and the tracks and chains are checked for proper alignment.

5 Final checks are then performed to ensure that motorized parts are functioning properly, the belts and chains are moving smoothly and at the correct speed, and the emergency braking system is activated. The step treads must be far enough apart so that they do not rub against one another. However, they should be positioned in such a way that no large gaps are present. Such gaps could be a source of injury.

Quality Control

The Code of Federal Regulations (CFR) contains guidelines for escalator quality control and establishes minimum inspection standards. Standard 29CFR1917.116 states, "Elevators and escalators shall be thoroughly inspected at intervals not exceeding one year. Additional monthly inspections for satisfactory operation shall be conducted by designated persons." The government further requires records of annual inspections to be posted near the escalator or to be available at the site. The escalator's maximum load limit also has to be posted and not exceeded.

All escalators in the United States that are manufactured and installed comply with the safety code set by the American National Standards Institutes and published by the American Society of Mechanical Engineers (ASME). The ASME A17.1 Code requires the regular inspection of escalators by specially trained and qualified inspectors. These inspectors are usually employees of a state office. In addition, escalator owners generally contract with escalator maintenance companies to conduct regular maintenance. However, escalator accidents continue to occur due to poorly maintained equipment. Some of the more severe accidents involve entrapments, in which a rider's clothing or shoe gets caught between the step and the comb plate.

The Future

The escalator industry continues to develop products that meet the changing needs of the marketplace. Some of the newly developed designs include an escalator that can transport wheelchairs and a spiral escalator that increases usable spaces by its installation in the corners or at the sides of large rooms. A new design is the high-rise escalator that can go up to over 100 feet and is being installed in underground train and bus stations, as well as in airports and convention centers.

For More Information

Web Sites

"Escalator Safety." *Elevator World, Inc.* http://www.elevator-world.com/magazine/archive01/9812-005.htm (accessed on July 22, 2002).

"Multi-Directional Movement of Passengers." *The Museum for the Preservation of Elevating History.* http://www.theelevatormuseum.org/f/f.htm (accessed on July 22, 2002).

Roberts, William A. "Take me UP to the Ballgame." *Elevator World, Inc.* http://www.elevator-world.com/magazine/archive01/9906-004.html-ssi (accessed on July 22, 2002).

Football

*In 1892,
Spaulding Sports
Worldwide in
Chicopee,
Massachusetts,
produced the first
American-made
football.*

A football, as defined in the United States by the National Football League (NFL), is a ball that "shall be made of an inflated rubber bladder enclosed in a pebble-grained, leather case. It shall have the form of a prolate spheroid (an oval shape)." The game of football is played between two teams of eleven members each on a one-hundred-yard rectangular field with a goal post at each end. The object of the game is to advance the ball over the opponent's goal line for a touchdown.

The ancient Greeks played a version of football called *harpaston*. The game took place on a rectangular field with goal lines on both ends. A center line divided two teams made up of equal numbers of players of different sizes. The *harpaston*, or handball, was thrown into the air, and the players tried to pass, kick, or run the ball past the opposing team's goal line. The ancient Romans played a similar game, calling it *harpastum*. During the 1100s, the English were known to have played a variety of football called *mellay*, from which the word "melee" came. Appropriately named, the game, played with no rules of any kind, resembled a violent, noisy, confused fighting. The players used an inflated pig bladder for a ball. During the 1500s, natives of Florence, Italy, played *calcio*, a kicking game not unlike modern-day football.

During the seventeenth and eighteenth centuries, students in exclusive schools in England, such as Eton, Rugby, Harrow, and Winchester, played a soccer-like version of football, with the players kicking the ball. Legend has it that in 1823, the game of football changed when a certain Rugby player caught the ball and ran with it across the opponents' goal line. Soon after the game was given the name rugby after the school.

American football

The first English people who settled in the United States brought a football game resembling soccer to North America. Settlers in Virginia played this form of football during the early 1600s, using a bladder, or an inflatable bag, filled with air. However, it took another two hundred years before the game became popular in colleges.

During the second half of the 1800s, college students played different versions of soccer and rugby. The first intercollegiate game was played in 1869 between Rutgers College (New Brunswick, New Jersey) and Princeton University (Princeton, New Jersey). Twenty-five players comprised each team. Patterned after the English sport of soccer, the game used a round rubber ball. Any throwing of the ball or running with it was prohibited. Instead, the ball was moved by dribbling or batting with the hand or fist. The team scoring the first six goals would be the winner. Rutgers won six to four.

Brett Favre, quarterback for the Green Bay Packers, was named the NFL's Most Valuable Player for three consecutive years in the late 1990s. *Reproduced by permission of AP/Wide World Photos.*

In 1874, Harvard University (Cambridge, Massachusetts) invited McGill University (Montreal, Canada) to play football. The teams agreed to play two games: One game following soccer rules, the second game following rugby rules and using an oval ball. Different colleges started adopting the rugby-type football, in which the oval ball was advanced by running and kicking. Each team consisted of fifteen players. This was the beginning of American football.

Football games usually got violent due to the absence of rules. Since the players did not wear protective uniforms or head covers, serious

bladder: The inflatable part of a football that looks like a bag.

butyl rubber: An artificial rubber that is resistant to tearing and the effects of sunlight or chemicals.

injuries were common. In the early 1880s, Walter Camp (1859–1925), a Yale University coach, recommended the first rules for American football. He was responsible for reducing the number of players from fifteen to eleven per team. Camp also introduced the line of scrimmage, a system of downs, the point system of scoring, and the quarterback position.

Playing by the rules

In 1905, it was reported that several high school and college students had died as a result of playing the violent game of football. The following year, coaches agreed to establish rules, forming what is now known as the National Collegiate Athletic Association (NCAA). Over the years, the rules of the game continued to change. In 1912, the NCAA changed the circumference of the ball from 27 inches (68.6 centimeters) to 23 inches (58.4 centimeters).

In 1920, the American Professional Football Association was formed, and professional football began. This organization became the National Football League (NFL) in 1922.

Raw Materials

During the early days of football, a pig's bladder was inflated and used as the ball. Today's football, although called pigskin, is not made from any part of a pig. It is made of cowhide, which is durable and can be easily tanned to make leather.

Design

The football's oval shape makes it hard to catch and hold and also causes unpredictable bounces. White raised lacing, consisting of eight stitches, helps the players grip the ball. There have been attempts to change the football's design. For example, dimples on the ball have been tried. These proved to be impractical because dirt and mud tended to get caught in the indentations.

The Manufacturing Process

The manufacture of a football involves numerous steps, with quality-control checks at different points of production.

die: A mold for cutting leather into football-shaped panels.

down: One of four consecutive plays in which a team must either score or advance the ball at least ten yards to keep possession of the ball.

industrial sewing machine: A sewing machine that is bigger and more powerful than a regular home sewing machine.

prolate: Elongated at the opposite ends.

With the increasing popularity of football, tossing a football around in the yard has become as frequent a sight as playing catch with a baseball. *Photograph by Kelly A. Quin. Copyright © Kelly A. Quin. Reproduced by permission of the photographer.*

1 The part of the cowhide called the bend undergoes special tanning processes, or chemical procedures by which raw hide is converted to leather. The bend is chosen because it is the thickest and strongest part of the cowhide. This is the hide that is taken from the area just below the shoulder and covers the upper back of the animal.

2 The bend is cut using a hydraulically-driven clicking machine, a machine powered by water under pressure. The powerful machine with football-shaped metal dies (molds) cuts four panels of leather at the same time.

3 Each leather panel goes through a skiving machine that trims the leather to the required thickness and weight.

4 A synthetic (artificial) lining is sewn to each panel using an industrial sewing machine. The lining, which is made up of three layers

skiving machine: A machine that trims the leather to the required thickness and weight.

spheroid: A ball.

tanning: The chemical process by which animal hide and skin are converted into leather.

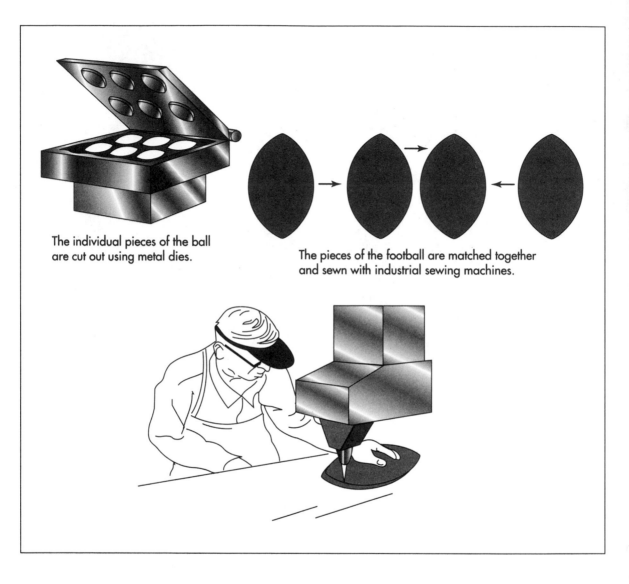

The individual pieces of the ball are cut out using metal dies.

The pieces of the football are matched together and sewn with industrial sewing machines.

of fabric cemented together, prevents the ball from stretching or growing out of shape during use.

5 Areas of the ball that will have the lacing holes and the hole for the inflating needle receive a facing, or an additional piece of material for protection. The holes are then punched.

6 The four leather panels are sewn together inside-out using a hot-wax lockstitch sewing machine. A lockstitch is a double-thread stitch that locks the top and bottom threads together, so that pulling

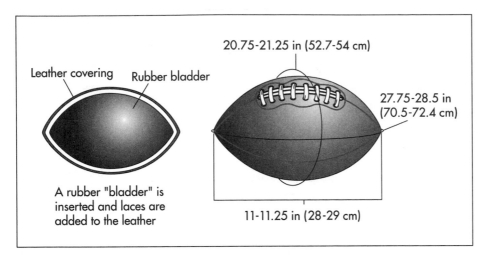

Leather covering   Rubber bladder

20.75-21.25 in (52.7-54 cm)

27.75-28.5 in (70.5-72.4 cm)

A rubber "bladder" is inserted and laces are added to the leather

11-11.25 in (28-29 cm)

A two-layer butyl rubber bladder is inserted, the ball is laced, and then it is inflated with a pressure of not less than 12.5 lb (6 kg) but no more than 13.5 lb (6.1 kg). Measurements shown are specific to footballs manufactured by Wilson.

a thread would not unravel the seam. After the stitching is finished, the ball is turned right-side out.

7 A two-layer butyl rubber bladder is inserted and the ball is laced. It is then inflated with air pressure of not less than 12.5 pounds (6 kilograms) but no more than 13.5 pounds (6.1 kilograms). After inflation, the ball is checked for its required size and weight.

8 The ball is branded with the manufacturer's name and number.

9 After final inspections, the balls are boxed and shipped to designated schools and ball clubs.

Quality Control

The manufacture of a football involves special skills and attention to details. For example, at the Wilson Football Factory (Ada, Ohio) of the Wilson Sporting Goods Company, each football is hand-made. The company has employees whose main job is to turn the footballs right-side out. The process has been compared to "turning a sneaker inside out." The employees use steam boxes to make the leather softer and easier to work with. They also use a vertical steel bar to help in turning the sewed leather panels.

Quality checks are performed at each stage of production. Inspectors make sure that the Wilson football, the NFL's official ball since 1941, weighs between 14 and 15 ounces (397 and 425.25 grams). The ball must measure 20.75 to 21.25 inches (52.7 to 54 centimeters) around the middle and 27.75 to 28.5 inches (70.5 to 72.4 centimeters) around its ends. The required measurement from tip to tip is 11 to 11.25 inches (28 to 29 centimeters).

The Future

Changes to the football are more likely to be in materials rather than design. The goal is a ball that has a "broken-in" feel right out of the box. A new type of cover material is called composite leather. It is a blend of synthetic (artificial) materials that are made to resemble and feel like leather. The synthetic materials typically consist of a plastic polyurethane and a microfiber (a type of polyester) backing. The football is lightweight, does not retain as much water as a leather ball, is less likely to get hard during cold weather, and is easier to grip.

For More Information

Books

Anderson, Dave. *The Story of Football.* Revised ed. New York, NY: Beech Tree Books, 1997.

Buckley, James, Jr. *Football.* New York, NY: DK Publishing, Inc., 1999.

McComb, David G. *Sports: An Illustrated History.* New York, NY: Oxford University Press, Inc., 1998.

Whittingham, Richard. *Rites of Autumn: The Story of College Football.* New York, NY: The Free Press, 2001.

Web Sites

"Camp and His Followers: American Football 1876–1889." *Professional Football Researchers Association.* http://www.footballresearch.com/articles/frpage.cfm?topic=d-to1889 (accessed on July 22, 2002).

"The Making of a Football." *Wilson Sporting Goods Company.* http://www.wilsonsports.com/football/index.asp?content_id=783 (accessed on July 22, 2002).

Gas Mask

Reproduced by permission of AP/Wide World Photos.

A gas mask is a face-covering device designed to protect the wearer from inhaling harmful gases and other poisonous contaminants by filtering and purifying the inhaled air. Some gas masks give protection by supplying the wearer with a supply of fresh air. These are called air-supplied respirators, which may come as a self-contained, portable apparatus carried by the user on his or her back or as a device that connects to a stationary oxygen tank. The second type of gas mask is a face mask that is outfitted with a filter to screen out the contaminants and poisonous materials. This gas mask is known as an air-purifying respirator (APR) and will be discussed here. An APR consists of a tight-fitting face piece that contains one or more filter cartridges, an exhalation valve, and transparent (see-through) eyepieces.

Gas masks are used to filter many undesirable airborne substances, from industrial fumes gases used in chemical warfare.

The Morgan safety hood

Garrett Augustus Morgan (1877–1963), an African American inventor, obtained a patent for the first air-purifying respirator in 1914. Morgan described his invention as a "breathing device" for firemen so that they could breathe freely in a burning house, protected from the smoke and gases that could cause suffocation. The device was an airtight canvas hood worn over the head. It was connected to double breathing tubes that merged into a single tube at the back. The open end had a sponge soaked with water for filtering the smoke and for cooling the air that entered the hood. Morgan also intended the device to be used by people who work

Gas masks and protective clothing are part of the uniform for municipal employees who participate in anti-chemical training exercises. *Reproduced by permission of AP/Wide World Photos.*

activated charcoal: A highly adsorbent carbon in powder or granular form and used as a filter by collecting impurities on its surface.

catalyst: A substance that speeds up a chemical reaction, but does not itself undergo the chemical reaction.

with harmful fumes or dust, such as chemists and engineers. Firemen in various large cities in New York, Pennsylvania, and Ohio used the device, which they called the Morgan helmet or safety hood.

In 1916, Morgan's gas mask proved very valuable when an explosion trapped several workers in a tunnel at the Cleveland Water Works more than two hundred feet below Lake Erie. Morgan and his brother Frank put on gas masks and went down the tunnel to save about twenty workers from the smoke, dust, and poisonous gases that had filled the tunnel. During World War I (1914–18), Morgan's gas mask was used by American soldiers as protection against chemicals, such as chlorine, phosgene, and mustard gases, used in warfare.

Modern gas masks

Over the years, significant advances in gas mask technology have occurred, especially in the area of new filtration aids. Masks have also

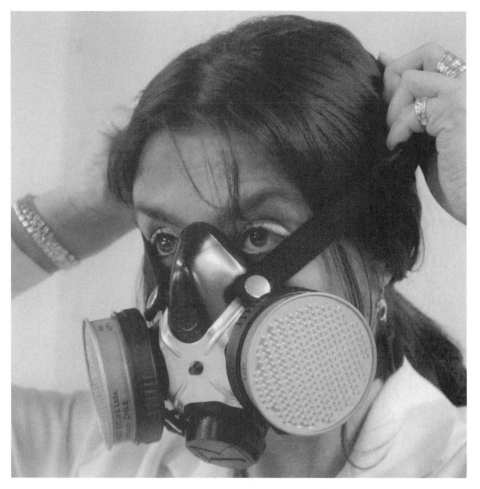

Gas masks help prevent the nose and mouth from inhaling toxic fumes. *Reproduced by permission of AP/Wide World Photos.*

contaminant: A substance that makes something unclean or impure.

filter: Carbon or any porous material used to screen impurities and harmful gases.

patent: A grant by a government to an inventor, assuring the inventor the sole right to make and sell his or her invention for a period of time.

reactant: A substance that causes a chemical reaction, at the same time taking part in that reaction.

sprue: The vertical channel in the injection-molding machine through which the melted plastic is poured.

thermoplastic: A type of plastic that can be reshaped at high temperatures.

been made more comfortable. In addition, modern plastic and silicone rubber compounds have produced a tighter fit. Today's masks have various designs. Some cover only the mouth and nose, while others cover the whole face, including the eyes.

Gas masks filter undesirable airborne substances, including toxic (poisonous) industrial fumes, vaporized paint, particulate pollution (dust, smoke, and soot from the burning of fuel), and gases used in chemical warfare. Masks may be used for military or industrial purposes. Although they share the same design, military gas masks have to satisfy standards that are different from those used in industry. This article discusses the manufacture of the full-face gas mask used in industry.

Raw Materials

A full-face mask consists of a flexible face-covering piece, transparent eye lenses, a filter cartridge, and a series of straps and bands to hold the device snugly in place. The face-covering piece, also called the skirt of the mask, covers from roughly the hairline to below the chin. It holds the other parts in place and provides a secure seal around the face area. The exhalation device may be inserted in the face piece. This one-way valve lets exhaled air out without allowing outside air to enter the mask.

The transparent eye lenses protect the wearer's vision. They are made of chemically resistant, clear polycarbonate plastic. Depending on the industry in which the gas mask will be used, the eyepieces may be specially treated to screen out certain types of light. Some masks may be made shatterproof or fog-resistant. Most eyepieces are made by outside suppliers and then shipped to the mask manufacturer for assembly.

The filter cartridge is a styrene plastic canister 3 to 4 inches (8 to 10 centimeters) across and 1 inch (2.5 centimeters) deep. The canister contains a filtration aid. Carbon-based filters are commonly used because they tend to adsorb (collect on their surfaces) large amounts of organic gases, such as those released by paints, varnishes, and fuels. However, carbon generally does not adsorb inorganic vapors well. To enable or "activate" carbon to adsorb inorganic vapors, the adsorptive properties of carbon are boosted by incorporating certain reactants or catalysts into the porous (having holes) carbon particles. Both reactants and catalysts bring on chemical reaction in the particles, the former by taking part in the reaction, and the latter by speeding it up without itself undergoing the chemical reaction.

The type of activated carbon used in the filter cartridge depends on the type of industrial contaminant that needs to be screened. For example, carbon treated with a combination of molybdenum and triethylenediamine is used to screen out hydrogen cyanide, cyanogen chloride, and formaldehyde. Hydrogen cyanide and cyanogen chloride are hazardous chemicals emitted during such industrial processes as petroleum refining and metal

German-made gas masks and Israeli-made gas masks on sale at an outdoor supply store in Hermiston, Oregon. *Reproduced by permission of AP/Wide World Photos.*

ore processing. They are also used in the production of dyes, acrylic plastics, and pharmaceuticals (drugs). Formaldehyde, on the other hand, is used widely in the manufacture of building materials and household products, including disinfectants and fumigants (for killing pests). Carbon that is treated with sodium, potassium, and other alkalis is used to adsorb sewage vapors (hydrogen sulfide), chlorine, and other harmful gases. Other types of activated carbon use silver or oxides of iron and zinc to trap contaminants.

The elastic straps that hold the gas mask to the face are made of silicone rubber, a type of synthetic (artificial) rubber that can withstand high temperature and is highly resistant to many chemicals. Additional straps may be used in the mask to allow it to be comfortably hung around the neck when not in use.

Design

The design of the gas mask depends on the industrial environment in which it will be used. Some masks are designed with speech diaphragms (thin membranes in the mouthpieces that allow for communication).

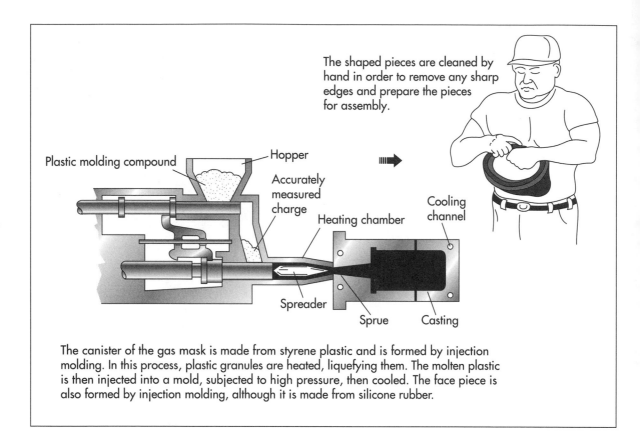

The shaped pieces are cleaned by hand in order to remove any sharp edges and prepare the pieces for assembly.

Plastic molding compound

Hopper

Accurately measured charge

Heating chamber

Cooling channel

Spreader

Sprue

Casting

The canister of the gas mask is made from styrene plastic and is formed by injection molding. In this process, plastic granules are heated, liquefying them. The molten plastic is then injected into a mold, subjected to high pressure, then cooled. The face piece is also formed by injection molding, although it is made from silicone rubber.

Some are designed to accept additional filters, while others are made so that they can be attached to an external air supply. Based on the intended use of the mask, the filter that is used may vary.

The Manufacturing Process

Different styles of gas masks are used in different industries, depending on the type of protection the wearer needs. The manufacturing steps discussed here relate to full-faced gas masks that are used for protection against high concentrations of toxic materials.

Canister

1 The filter canister is made from styrene plastic, which is especially suited for the process called injection molding. During this process, an accurately measured charge (the styrene granules) is fed from the hopper holding the granules into the injection-molding machine.

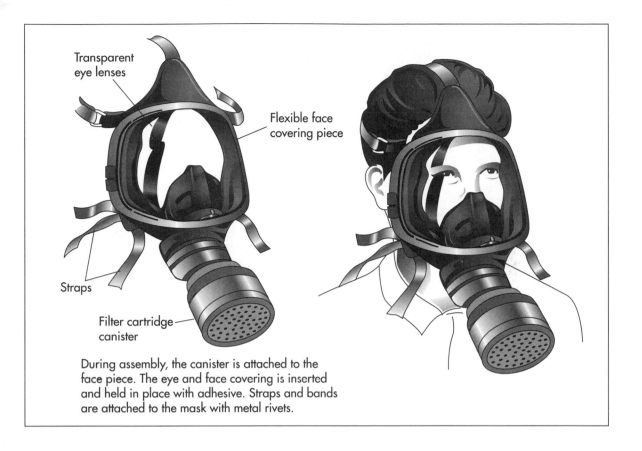

Transparent eye lenses

Flexible face covering piece

Straps

Filter cartridge canister

During assembly, the canister is attached to the face piece. The eye and face covering is inserted and held in place with adhesive. Straps and bands are attached to the mask with metal rivets.

The granules melt at very high temperature and are poured through a vertical passage in the mold called the sprue. The mold used for the canister consists of two disk-shaped metal pieces that are clamped together. The liquid plastic is injected into the mold cavity using great pressure. Casting, or the forming of the solid canister parts from melted plastic, occurs as cold water is circulated within the cooling channels in the mold. The formed solid plastics are released from the molds, trimmed, and cleaned.

Styrene is an ideal material for injection molding because it is a thermoplastic, which means that it can be repeatedly melted and reshaped at high temperatures. This also means that scrap pieces remaining from the process can be reworked to make additional canisters. As a result, very little styrene is wasted. In addition, styrene remains stable and does not undergo chemical changes when remelted and resolidified (made solid) during cooling. It is also resistant to water and chemicals.

2 Injection molding is also used to produce small circular screens that fit inside the canister. The screens are designed to hold the activated carbon in place inside the canister. As the canisters travel down the assembly line, a screen is inserted, a filtering material is put in place, and a second screen is attached.

Face-covering piece

3 The face-covering piece is also created using injection molding. Like styrene, silicon rubber that is used for the face piece is a thermoplastic that can be remelted and reshaped as needed. It also conforms to the curves in the face and head. After the molded face piece has cooled and hardened, the rough edges must be cleaned off by hand before the other components can be attached to it.

Final assembly

4 The mask components are assembled on a partially automated assembly line with two to four workers supervising the process. The completed filter canister is attached to the face piece. The eye lenses are inserted and held in place with adhesive. Then, the straps and bands are attached to the face piece with metal rivets (fasteners). Finally, the gas mask is given a final inspection.

Packaging

5 After the gas masks are inspected, they are identified with markings as specified by the American National Standard for Identification of Air Purifying Respirator Cartridges and Canisters. The completed masks are then packaged for shipping. The container must clearly identify the type of mask in the package. In addition, the containers must be so designed that they allow easy access in case of emergency.

Gas masks are rigorously tested in laboratories to make sure they are effective before they are released for sale. *Reproduced by permission of AP/Wide World Photos.*

Quality Control

The raw materials, including the filters and plastic granules (styrene and silicone rubber), are inspected when they are first received at the manufacturing site. The finished eyepieces that are manufactured by an outside company are also examined. The canister is tested after it is put together to make sure it has proper seal and that the carbon filter works. The mask is inspected after all the parts have been assembled. Finally, the complete gas mask may be placed on a mannequin head to ensure the seal is tight and that it maintains its seal during movements.

The federal government regulates the types of gas masks that must be used in specific industrial environments. The National Institute of Occupational Safety and Health (NIOSH) is the government agency that tests gas masks. Mask types that are recognized by the federal government include self-contained breathing apparatus, the non-powered air purifying particulate respirators, chemical cartridge respirators, and dust masks. Federal regulations also specify the type of testing that must be performed based on the contaminants for which the masks have been designed. Testing includes exposing the masks to the contaminant for long periods of time and subjecting them to certain temperature and humidity conditions. Then, the amount of time it takes the contaminant to saturate and penetrate the filter is measured.

The Future

The basic design of the gas mask is not likely to change since it has been tested numerous times over the past several decades. Future gas masks will rely on advances in the materials used, which will result in smaller and more lightweight products. Research is also being conducted in creating carbon filters that are more effective and smaller in size.

For More Information

Periodicals

Scheel, Ken. "The Positive Side of Respirators." *Occupational Hazards* (April 2000): pp. 67–68; p. 70.

Web Sites

"Garrett Augustus Morgan." *U.S. Department of Transportation.* http://education.dot.gov/aboutmorgan.html (accessed on July 22, 2002).

"Respirator Basics." *NASA's Occupational Health Program.* http://ohp.ksc.nasa.gov/disciplines/env-health/rpbasics.html (accessed on July 22, 2002).

Gasoline

Gasoline is a volatile (evaporates quickly), flammable (readily burns) liquid obtained from the refining (purifying) of petroleum, or crude oil. Almost all gasoline produced is used to fuel automobiles. A small percentage is used to power farm equipment and airplanes.

The United States is the world's leading consumer of petroleum. In 2001, Americans consumed over nineteen million barrels of oil per day.

Underground treasure

Scientists are not sure how petroleum is formed, but most believe that it is formed from the remains of tiny plants and animals called plankton. According to this theory, millions of years ago these plankton lived on the surfaces of the oceans that covered a large part of the earth. When they died, they sank to the bottom of the ocean where they were covered by mud and sediments, or materials that had settled to the ocean bottom. Over the years, this process was repeated until the extreme pressure and heat from the sediments turned the plankton remains into petroleum and natural gas. It is believed that the crude oil and gas seeped upward into porous rocks (rocks with pores, or small holes). Solid rocks eventually formed around the porous rocks, trapping the oil and gas within them.

Some scientists do not believe that crude oil deposits come from formerly living things subjected to great heat and pressure for millions of years. They believe that crude oil deposits were created when the planet Earth was being formed and that many of these reservoirs are as yet untapped.

Since the beginning of civilization, people have recovered the oil that seeped through the earth's surface and put it to use. They used it for waterproofing their clothing and for caulking (patching up cracks) ships and artificial waterways. They also used it as a lubricant and medicine.

The first oil well

On August 27, 1859, Edwin L. Drake (1819–1880) struck oil near Titusville, Pennsylvania, at a depth of 69.5 feet (21.2 meters). This accomplishment could not have come at a better time. Whale oil that was used for lighting was getting more expensive due to scarcity, and people were looking for a cheaper lamp fuel. Prior to Drake's oil discovery, several scientists had already found ways of producing kerosene from the crude oil that seeped out of certain rock formations.

Soon, oil wells were being drilled in the Titus region, as well as in other states, including Ohio, California, Texas, and Oklahoma. One of the biggest oil wells drilled occurred in Spindletop, Texas, on January 10, 1901. Observers claimed that the well spewed oil about 100 feet (30 meters) higher than the 64-foot (19.5-meter) derrick (the support structure surrounding the drilling equipment). The oil continued to flow out of the well for nine days. That tremendous oil find was the start of the American oil industry.

Gasoline and automobiles

When crude oil was originally refined to make kerosene, gasoline

On January 10, 1901, drillers struck an oil well in Spindletop, Texas, which produced about 100,000 barrels (4.2 million gallons or 15.9 million liters) of oil per day. *Reproduced by permission of UPI/Corbis-Bettmann.*

was also produced. At first, people tried to use gasoline for lamp fuel, but the explosion that followed such use quickly discouraged the practice. Gasoline was considered of no value and was therefore thrown away. However, the invention of gasoline-powered engines to run the newly invented automobile made gasoline a very valuable product.

In 1883, German engineer Gottlieb Daimler (1834–1900) invented an engine that ran on gasoline. Four years later, he used this gasoline engine in a four-wheeled vehicle. His automobile traveled at a speed of eleven miles per hour. In 1899, Daimler produced the first Mercedes automobile, named after his daughter. Daimler's engine has been the model for almost all automobiles manufactured since the late nineteenth century. The first American car powered by gasoline was built in Chicopee, Massachusetts, by Charles Duryea (1861–1938) and his brother, J. Frank (1869–1967), in 1893.

How much petroleum do we use?

Petroleum supplies more energy to the world today than any other source. The United States is the world's leading consumer of petroleum. In 2001, Americans consumed over nineteen million barrels of oil per day. That same year, the United States had an estimated oil supply of just nine million barrels per day. That means that the nation had to import additional oil to meet the public demand.

bit: A metal tool attached to a rotary drill and used for breaking up rock formations under the earth's surface.

Christmas tree: A pyramid-like structure consisting of control valves, nozzles, and pressure gauges and installed at the top of a well to control the flow of oil at the completion of the drilling.

Raw Materials

Gasoline is one of the products derived from the distillation and refining of crude oil. Gasoline first has to be separated from the other components through a process called fractional distillation (see below) and then refined and treated with additives to improve its quality. Other chemicals are also added to gasoline to further stabilize it and improve its color and smell in a process called "sweetening."

The Manufacturing Process

The manufacture of gasoline is a complex process. Separating the gasoline fraction (part) from crude oil is just the first step in the process.

To produce gasoline of good quality, manufacturers experiment with different combinations of ingredients and additives.

Exploration

1 The first step in the manufacture of gasoline is to find its parent ingredient, crude oil. Sometimes, the presence of oil leakages or of certain sedimentary rocks indicates the possible presence of oil. If obvious signs of oil reservoirs are absent, oil exploration is undertaken.

Oil prospectors, people who explore an area for the presence of oil, may examine the surface characteristics of an area and take pictures of these features. They may set off explosives underground and then analyze the resulting shock waves to determine the rock type and depth. Some explorers use devices to measure the gravity and magnetic field of rock formations, which tend to differ depending on the presence of oil deposits. Others study sound waves that bounce off rocks below the earth's surface, providing information about the types of rocks underground.

2 After a possible oil reservoir is found, core samples are taken from test wells using a drill. These samples of the underground layers of the earth are analyzed to confirm the presence of oil. Chemical tests are also performed to determine if further drilling should be done.

Gas stations have popped up on the corner of almost every intersection in America, giving consumers easy access to fill-ups. *Reproduced by permission of Corbis Corporation.*

core sample: A sample of underground mud that is drilled and analyzed for the presence of oil.

gusher: An oil well that flows freely and abundantly as a result of natural gas pressure.

kerosene: A fuel produced during the breaking down of crude oil into its parts. It is used for cooking, heating, and lighting.

knocking: The sound and the damage caused by the premature burning of gasoline in the engine cylinder.

Drilling

3 Crude oil is obtained through wells that can be as deep as 1,000 feet (305 meters). Rotary drilling is the method most commonly used to make holes in the ground. A tower-like steel framework called a derrick is constructed over the site where the well will be dug. This framework holds the drilling equipment. The drill bit, a large circular metal cutting tool fitted with teeth, is attached to a hollow pipe. As the pipe turns, the drill bit spins, cutting through the subsoil (soil below the earth's surface) and hard rock layers. More pipes are added to the equipment top as the bit digs deeper.

A heavy liquid mixture called "mud" is poured down the pipe to keep the drill bit from overheating. The mud also carries crushed rock pieces to the surface, keeps the well wall from collapsing, and prevents oil from "gushing" should the bit reach an oil reservoir. When the oil reservoir is reached, the mud's weight keeps the oil from escaping uncontrollably. The drill is removed and the well is sealed with a contraption called a "Christmas tree," a pyramid-like structure consisting of valves, nozzles, and pressure gauges that control the flow of oil.

Recovery

4 To remove the oil from the well, a complicated system of pipes and valves is installed directly into the drilling well. The natural pressure in the reservoir rock forces the oil out of the well and into the pipes. The pipes are connected to a recovery system, which consists of a series of larger pipes that transport the oil to the refinery by first passing through an oil (liquid) and gas (nonliquid) separator. The refinery is the industrial factory where crude oil is separated into its various parts and converted to usable products.

5 Eventually, the natural pressure in the rock reservoir decreases. However, great quantities of oil may still remain in the rock formation. To recover the rest of the oil, pressure is restored using water. Holes are drilled around the perimeter of the well, and water is then added, flooding the well. This causes the crude oil to float on the water. Another recovery method involves injecting carbon dioxide gas into the pocket above the oil deposit, thereby pushing out the oil. Some drillers use chemicals or steam to force more oil from the reservoir rock.

Offshore oil drilling platforms, like this one off the coast of Texas, are a huge source of oil, getting it from deep beneath the ocean floor. *Reproduced by permission of Photo Researchers, Inc.*

Fractional distillation

6 Crude oil that comes out of the ground cannot be used in its natural form. It has to be separated into its different parts, or fractions, by a process called distillation, which is performed in a fractional distillation column. During distillation, the crude oil components are separated according to molecular weight.

The crude oil is first pumped into a furnace and heated to over 600 degrees Fahrenheit (316 degrees Centigrade), causing it to evaporate (change from liquid to vapor). The vapors enter the bottom of a fractional distillation column (a huge tower fitted with a series of horizontal trays) and rise through the column. The lightest vapors, which rise to the top of the column, condense (change back to liquid) and settle on the different levels of trays throughout the length of the tower. Gasoline, having a low molecular weight, condenses at the top of the column and is one of the first fractions drawn off.

natural gas: A gas that occurs in nature, usually with petroleum, and believed to have been formed by the actions of extreme pressure and heat on buried plankton millions of years ago.

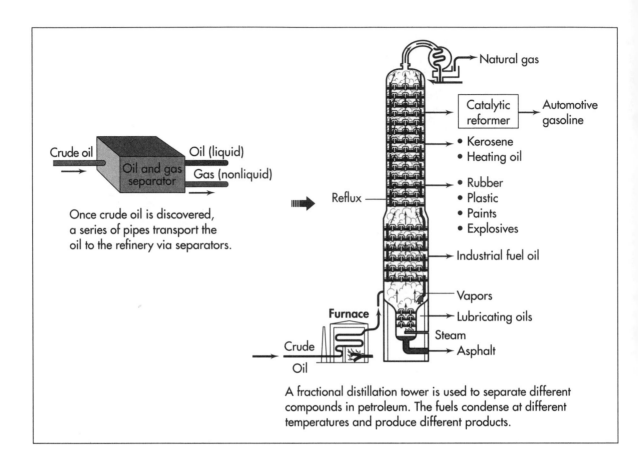

Crude oil → **Oil and gas separator** → Oil (liquid) / Gas (nonliquid) →

Once crude oil is discovered, a series of pipes transport the oil to the refinery via separators.

→ Natural gas

Catalytic reformer → Automotive gasoline

- Kerosene
- Heating oil

- Rubber
- Plastic
- Paints
- Explosives

Reflux

→ Industrial fuel oil

→ Vapors
→ Lubricating oils

Furnace

Crude Oil

Steam
→ Asphalt

A fractional distillation tower is used to separate different compounds in petroleum. The fuels condense at different temperatures and produce different products.

Fractional distillation itself does not produce gasoline from crude oil. It is just the first step in separating the crude oil fractions. Further refining processes are later used to improve the quality of the raw gasoline.

Refining crude oil fractions

octane number/rating: A measure of the ability of a gasoline to prevent engine knocking. Gasolines with a higher octane rating are less likely to cause knocking.

In order to increase the amount of gasoline produced from crude oil, thermal cracking is used. Thermal cracking cracks, or breaks down, the heavier parts of crude oil by subjecting them to intense heat and high pressure. In the past, only 10 percent of crude oil produced gasoline. With thermal cracking, this proportion has been increased more than four times.

Other refining processes include catalytic cracking and polymerization. In catalytic cracking, the combination of heat and a catalyst (a substance that causes or speeds up a chemical reaction without itself being changed), such as aluminum, platinum, processed clay, and acids, breaks down the larger molecules of crude oil into gasoline. Polymerization is the opposite of cracking. In this process, the smaller molecules of crude oil are combined to form gasoline.

Additives

8 After gasoline is refined, antiknock additives are added to react with the chemicals in gasoline to prevent "engine knock." Knocking is the sound and the damage caused by the premature burning of gasoline in the combustion chamber of the internal-combustion engine. Antiknock compounds added include tertiary-butyl alcohol and methyl tertiary-butyl ether.

Other additives include antioxidants, which prevent the formation of gum in the engine. Gum is a substance formed in gasoline that can coat the internal engine parts, causing damage.

Rating gasoline

9 Gasoline is primarily a mixture of two volatile liquids, heptane and isooctane. Pure heptane, a lighter fuel, burns so quickly that it produces a great amount of knocking in the engine. Pure isooctane burns slowly and produces almost no knocking. The higher the percentage of octane in gasoline, the less knocking occurs. Octane ratings measure the ability of a certain gasoline to prevent knocking. For example, an octane rating of 87 means that the gasoline

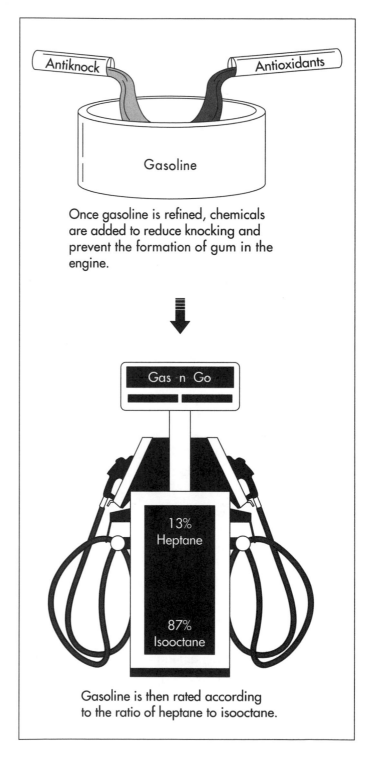

Once gasoline is refined, chemicals are added to reduce knocking and prevent the formation of gum in the engine.

Gasoline is then rated according to the ratio of heptane to isooctane.

mixture contains 87 percent isooctane and 13 percent heptane. The higher the octane rating or number, the less likely it is for the gasoline to cause knocking.

Quality Control

Drilling for crude oil is a complex process. Quality control involves using the latest technology that not only preserves the environment but also reduces the drilling time, considered the most expensive part of oil exploration.

Refineries have to meet U.S. Environmental Protection Agency (EPA) regulations in managing the various processes involved in gasoline manufacture. These include the storage of crude oil, intermediate products, and finished products. They also include the discharge of chemical pollutants into the air and the disposal of waste products, such as wastewater, incinerator ash, and used filters and catalysts.

plankton: Tiny plants and animals found in bodies of water.

refining: The process by which petroleum is purified and converted into a useful product, such as gasoline.

reservoir rock: A porous rock formation containing a significant amount of oil and/or natural gas and typically enclosed by nonporous rocks that have prevented the oil from escaping.

The Future

Petroleum, or crude oil, the source of gasoline, is a nonrenewable resource. Once it is used, it cannot be replaced. Today, crude oil provides about 97 percent of transportation fuels in the United States. Because gasoline is derived from a limited supply of petroleum, scientists are researching other sources of energy that could power cars.

One area of research involves different types of fuel cells that would replace the car engine. A fuel cell is basically a device that converts hydrogen fuel into electricity. Essentially, a fuel cell is a battery with an external fuel source—hydrogen—that continually recharges it. Scientists point out that fuel cells produce no pollution since their byproduct is water. Vehicles powered by fuel cells are currently being tested in different countries.

Scientists have also been looking for other sources of energy, including steam power used in steamboats of the past. Electric cars have been developed, and wind energy is also powering cars.

In the meantime, the petroleum industry continues to develop advanced technology in drilling for oil. In the Gulf of Mexico, computers are being used to direct drilling operations almost two miles beneath the surface of the water. Drills are fitted with computers that transmit information about wells. Advanced diagnostic and imaging technology allows one to "see" oil and gas reservoir features to a certain point from the earth's surface. Scientists are also looking into using high-intensity lasers for drilling.

For More Information

Books

Aaseng, Nathan. *Business Builders in Oil.* Minneapolis, MN: The Oliver Press, 2000.

Bredeson, Carmen. *The Spindletop Gusher: The Story of the Texas Oil Boom.* Brookfield, CT: The Mill Press, 1996.

Periodicals

Hart, David. "Fueling the Future." *New Scientist.* (June 16, 2001): pp. 1–5.

Peters, Eric. "Premium Gas." *Consumers' Research Magazine.* (September 1998): pp. 1–2.

Web Sites

"Fuel Cells." *U.S. Department of Energy.* http://www.fueleconomy.gov/feg/fuelcell.shtml (accessed on July 22, 2002).

Index

A

AbioCor Implantable Replacement Heart *3:* 35, 37, 38 (ill.)
Achard, Franz *3:* 90
Achilles tendon *1:* 195
Acoustic guitar *1:* 109 (ill.)
Adams, Thomas *2:* 58, 63
Advanced Photo System (APS) *3:* 212–213
Aerodynamics *1:* 3, 118
Aerosol insecticide *3:* 197
Agitation *1:* 159
Air bag *2:* 1–10, 1 (ill.), 2 (ill.)
Air bag components *2:* 4 (ill.)
Air bag manufacturing *2:* 6 (ill.), 7 (ill.), 8 (ill.), 9 (ill.)
Air conditioner *3:* **1–10,** 1 (ill.), 3 (ill.), 5 (ill.)
Airframe *1:* 120
Air-purifying respirator (APR) *3:* 123
Airtime *3:* 219
Alcoke, Charles *3:* 215
Aldrin, Edwin E. "Buzz," Jr. *3:* 259
Alignment *1:* 73
"All You Need Is Love" *3:* 226
AlliedSignal *1:* 49
Allison, Doug *2:* 18
Alloy *1:* 123, 258, 274
Amati, Andrea *2:* 279
American National Standards Institute *1:* 97
Amplification *1:* 107
Anaheim Stadium *1:* 212 (ill.)
Angioplasty *2:* 16, 17 (ill.)
Angle of incidence *1:* 55
Animation *3:* **11–20,** 14 (ill.), 15 (ill.), 16 (ill.), 18 (ill.)
Annatto *1:* 58

Annealization *1:* 77, 259; *2:* 42
Anodization *1:* 123
Antibiotic *3:* **21–29,** 21 (ill.), 26 (ill.), 27 (ill.)
Antioxidants *1:* 156; *2:* 251
Anti-smoking poster *3:* 86 (ill.)
Apothecary *1:* 220
APS. *See* Advanced Photo System (APS)
Aramid *1:* 121
Arbor *2:* 70
Arc lamps *1:* 145
Archer, Frederick *3:* 206
Archive *1:* 55
Argon *2:* 9, 169–172, 175
Armstrong, Neil A. *3:* 259, 269
Aromatherapy *2:* 201
Aromatics *2:* 194
Arrays *1:* 211
Artificial heart *3:* **30–40,** 30 (ill.)
Asaho, Kunji *2:* 129 (ill.)
Assembly lines *1:* 1, 4 (ill.), 6 (ill.), 7 (ill.), 9 (ill.), 33; *2:* 109, 125, 218, 222, 237, 239
Atari Company *3:* 278
Atlantis *3:* 259 (ill.)
Attenuation *1:* 172
Audio encoding *1:* 81
Auréole *3:* 145
Autoclaves *1:* 123, 267
Autogiros *1:* 117
Automobile *1:* 1–11, 149, 229; *2:* 1, 3, 4, 36, 46, 75, 109, 120, 173, 176, 243, 247, 270
Avobenzone *2:* 251
Axles *1:* 4
Aztecs *1:* 46

Italic type indicates Series number; **boldface** type indicates main entries featured in Series 3; (ill.) indicates photographs and illustrations.

B

Baer, Ralph *3:* 278
Baird, John Logie *3:* 270–271
Bale chambers *2:* 104
Baler pickup *2:* 104
Ball bearings *1:* 260
Balloon *2:* 11–17, 11 (ill.), 12 (ill.), 17 (ill.), 38, 40, 50
Balloon manufacturing *2:* 14 (ill.), 15 (ill.)
Ballpoint pen *3:* **41–48,** 41 (ill.), 43 (ill.), 45 (ill.), 46 (ill.)
Balm *1:* 155
Banbury, Fernely H. *2:* 227
Banbury mixer *2:* 227
Bar code scanner *1:* 12–19, 13 (ill.), 16 (ill.), 17 (ill.)
Bar codes *1:* 12–19, 12 (ill.)
Barnard, Christiaan *3:* 31
Basalt *1:* 201
Base notes *2:* 200
Baseball *1:* 20–26, 20 (ill.), 21 (ill.), 25 (ill.); *2:* 19
Baseball construction *1:* 24 (ill.)
Baseball glove *2:* 18–25, 18 (ill.), 19 (ill.), 23 (ill.), 25 (ill.)
Baseball glove manufacturing *2:* 20 (ill.), 24 (ill.)
Baseball player *1:* 22 (ill.)
Bean bag plush toy *3:* **49–59,** 49 (ill.)
Bean bag plush toy manufacturing *3:* 55 (ill.), 56 (ill.)
Beanie Babies *3:* 49–51, 50 (ill.), 53 (ill.), 57
Bearings *1:* 142
Beatles, The *3:* 226
Bedrock *1:* 214
Beeper *2:* 26–35, 26 (ill.), 27 (ill.), 33 (ill.), 34 (ill.)
Beeper manufacturing *2:* 29 (ill.), 31 (ill.), 32 (ill.)
Bees *1:* 18
Beeswax *2:* 57, 62
Bell, Alexander Graham *1:* 172
"Bends" *3:* 267
Benz, Carl *1:* 2
Bergman, Torbern *3:* 247
Berthollet, Claude-Louis *2:* 87
Beryl *1:* 89

Berzelius, Jons Jakob *3:* 270
Besson, Gustave Auguste *1:* 258
Bevels *1:* 92
BIC pens *3:* 43
Bich, Marcel *3:* 43
Bicycle *2:* 36–47, 36 (ill.), 39 (ill.), 40 (ill.)
Bicycle components *2:* 41 (ill.), 45 (ill.)
Bicycle Museum of America *2:* 38
Bidermann, Samuel *2:* 213
Bifocals *1:* 90
Billet press *2:* 188
Binding *1:* 37, 44 (ill.)
Binoculars *1:* 90
Bionic *1:* 115
Biotin *1:* 166
Biro, Georg *3:* 42
Biro, Laszlo *3:* 42
Black box *3:* **60–69,** 60 (ill.), 61 (ill.), 67 (ill.)
Black powder *2:* 86, 89–92
Blackton, James Stuart *3:* 12
Blanking die *1:* 77
Blanking punch *1:* 275
Blister pack *1:* 78
Blow molding *2:* 242–244, 252, 253
Blow torch *1:* 261
Blown rubber *1:* 194
Blue jeans *1:* 27–35, 28 (ill.), 29 (ill.), 274
Blue jeans manufacturing *1:* 31 (ill.), 32 (ill.), 33 (ill.)
Blueprints *1:* 42
Bluhmel, Friedreich *1:* 257
Bombarding *2:* 174–176
Bomber jacket *3:* 155 (ill.)
Boneshaker bicycle *2:* 38
Book *1:* 36–45, 36 (ill.), 39 (ill.)
Bookmatching *1:* 109
Bores *1:* 243
Box camera advertisement *3:* 208 (ill.)
Box tubular valve *1:* 257
Box-stitching *1:* 52
Bradham, Caleb *3:* 247–248
Brady, Matthew *2:* 207
Braider *2:* 52
Braille *1:* 18; *2:* 270
Brass *1:* 255, 256; *2:* 21, 90, 91
Braun, Ferdinand Karl *3:* 270
Brigandine armor *1:* 47 (ill.)
British thermal units (BTU) *3:* 1

Broth *1:* 63
Broyage *1:* 69, 70
Bubble gum *2:* 57–59, 63, 65
Budding, Edwin *1:* 137
Bulb-wall blackening *1:* 150
Bullet resistant vest. *See* Bulletproof vest
Bulletproof vest *1:* 46–55, 46 (ill.), 50 (ill.), 54 (ill.)
Bulletproof vest production *1:* 53 (ill.)
Bulletproof vest testing *1:* 48
Bungee cord *2:* 48–56, 48 (ill.), 49 (ill.)
Bungee cord manufacturing *2:* 52 (ill.), 53 (ill.)
Bungee jumping *2:* 48, 49 (ill.), 50, 51, 54, 55 (ill.), 56
Burn-in *2:* 127, 219
Bushnell, Nolan *3:* 278
Butting *2:* 42
Buttons *1:* 272
Bynema *1:* 49

C

Cacahuatl *1:* 63
Cadmium *1:* 77
Calcio 3: 116
Calibration *1:* 245
Calotype *2:* 203; *3:* 205
Cam *1:* 75
Camera obscura 3: 204
Camera-ready *1:* 44
Cameras *1:* 90; *2:* 120, 127, 129, 202–207, 210–212
Camp, Walter *3:* 118
Candler, Asa *3:* 255
Candy *1:* 71
Carbon *1:* 121, 145
Carbon black *1:* 247
Carbon rubber *1:* 194
Carbonated water *3:* 247
Carding *1:* 30
Carnauba *1:* 155
Carrier, Willis *3:* 2
Cartwright, Alexander *1:* 20
Carver, George Washington *2:* 178, 179 (ill.)
Casing in *1:* 38
Casting *1:* 122; *2:* 136

CAT. *See* Computerized Axial Tomography (CAT)
Catcher's mitt *2:* 18
Cathode ray tube (CRT) *3:* 273 (ill.)
Catsup. *See* Ketchup
Cavity *1:* 256
Cayley, George *1:* 116
CD. *See* Compact disc (CD)
Cedar *2:* 187–189
Cello *2:* 279, 282
Cello guitar *1:* 108
Cellular phone *2:* 33, 35, 82, 84
Cellulose *2:* 205, 207
Cels (celluloids) *3:* 19
Celsius, Anders *1:* 239
Cement lasting *1:* 194
Central note *2:* 200
Centrifugal pump *2:* 75
Centrifuge *1:* 225; *2:* 15, 61
Cereal *3:* **70–78,** 70 (ill.), 71 (ill.), 76 (ill.)
Cereal manufacturing *3:* 73 (ill.), 74 (ill.)
Chain, Ernst *3:* 22
Chamois *1:* 192
Chandra X-ray Observatory *3:* 262
Changers *3:* 99
Charles, Jacques *2:* 11
Chassis *1:* 2
Cheese *1:* 56–62, 56 (ill.), 57 (ill.), 62 (ill.)
Cheese making *1:* 59 (ill.), 61 (ill.)
Chewing gum *2:* 57–65, 57 (ill.), 58 (ill.), 62 (ill.), 64 (ill.), 89, 191, 193, 194
Chewing gum manufacturing *2:* 60 (ill.), 61 (ill.), 63 (ill.)
Chicle *2:* 58–60, 63
Chip shooter *2:* 30
Chocalatl *1:* 63
Chocolate *1:* 63–72, 63 (ill.), 64 (ill.), 200; *2:* 100
Chocolate candy *1:* 67 (ill.)
Chocolate candy production *1:* 70 (ill.)
Chordophone *1:* 107
Christerson, Tom *3:* 38
Chromization *1:* 77
Chu, Grace *2:* 96
Cierva, Juan de la *1:* 117
Cigarette *3:* **79–88,** 79 (ill.), 80 (ill.), 83 (ill.), 86 (ill.)

Italic type indicates Series number; **boldface** type indicates main entries featured in Series 3; (ill.) indicates photographs and illustrations.

INDEX   **xi**

Italic type indicates Series number; **boldface** type indicates main entries featured in Series 3; (ill.) indicates photographs and illustrations.

INDEX **xiii**

Ford, Henry *1:* 1–2, 3 (ill.)
Forging *1:* 122
Formaldehyde *1:* 165
Fortrel EcoSpun *2:* 246, 247
Fortune cookie *2:* 96–101, 96 (ill.), 97 (ill.), 98 (ill.)
Fortune cookie manufacturing *2:* 99 (ill.), 100 (ill.)
Fractional distillation *2:* 169
Fragrances *2:* 193–196, 199–201
Frankincense *2:* 57, 194
Franklin, Benjamin *1:* 80 (ill.)
Freeblowing *1:* 124
French Harmless Hair Dye Company *3:* 145
Freon *2:* 2
Fresnel lens *2:* 265
Frets *1:* 107; *2:* 282
Friction inertial welding *2:* 6
Fuel cell *3:* 140
Functional testing *2:* 140
Fuselage *1:* 120

G

Galileo Galilei *1:* 238
Galleys *1:* 39
Galoshes *1:* 273
Galvanometer *1:* 210
Gama, Vasco da *1:* 219
Game Boy *3:* 279–280
Gas additives *3:* 139 (ill.)
Gas mask *3:* **123–131,** 123 (ill.), 124 (ill.), 125 (ill.), 127 (ill.)
Gas mask assembly *3:* 129 (ill.)
Gas mask manufacturing *3:* 128 (ill.)
Gas mask testing *3:* 130 (ill.)
Gas station *3:* 135 (ill.)
Gasoline *3:* **132–141,** 132 (ill.)
Geissler, Johann Heinrich Wilhelm *2:* 169
Gelatin *2:* 203, 204, 207, 209, 210
Gemini 3: 258
General Electric (GE) *2:* 131, 270
General Motors (GM) *2:* 51, 120, 124
Generator *1:* 94
Genovese *1:* 27
George Eastman House *2:* 205
Gerbach, A. *1:* 274

Germanium *1:* 14
Gershwin, George *2:* 216
Gertie the Dinosaur 3: 12, 13 (ill.)
Gibbon, John H. *3:* 31–32
Ginned cotton *1:* 30
Glass *1:* 84, 89; *2:* 67, 71, 162, 163, 169–176, 196, 198, 199, 203, 204, 241, 242, 247, 266
Glassblowing *1:* 241
Glue *1:* 229
Godwin, Linda *3:* 259 (ill.)
Gold *1:* 83; *2:* 206, 236
Goldenrod *1:* 41
Goldmark, Peter *3:* 271
Goldsmith, Michael *3:* 171
Golitsyn, Boris *1:* 210
Goodhue, Lyle *3:* 197
Goodyear, Charles *1:* 191, 247; *2:* 226
Gore closure *1:* 193
Gorie, John *3:* 2
Gortex *3:* 263
Graham, Sylvester *3:* 70
Granola *3:* 70
Granulator *1:* 227
GrapeNuts *3:* 71
Graphite *2:* 93, 186–191
Gravity Pleasure Road *3:* 215
Gravity Pleasure Switchback Railway *3:* 215
Gravure *1:* 42, 185
Gray, Laman *3:* 37
Gray, Thomas *1:* 210
Gridiron design *3:* 118
Grinding *1:* 94
Gruentzig, Andreas *2:* 16
Guarneri, Bartolomeo Giuseppe *2:* 279
Guitar *1:* 107–114, 107 (ill.), 109 (ill.), 113 (ill.); *2:* 279
Guitar manufacturing *1:* 111 (ill.)
Gum. *See* Chewing gum
Gumballs *2:* 62
Gunpowder *2:* 2, 86, 87, 89
Gutenberg, Johann *1:* 36

H

H. J. Heinz Company *2:* 162, 168
Hagiwara, Makoto *2:* 97
Hahn, Max *2:* 131

Italic type indicates Series number; **boldface** type indicates main entries featured in Series 3; (ill.) indicates photographs and illustrations.

INDEX **XV**

Ionization chamber smoke detectors
2: 233
IPLVAS *See* HeartMate Implantable
Pneumatic Left Ventricular Assist
System (IPLVAS)
Iron oxide *1:* 98
ISO. *See* International Standards Orga-
nization (ISO)

J

Jarvik, Robert *3:* 33 (ill.)
Jarvik-7 3: 31–32, 33 (ill.)
Jarvik-2000 Flowmaker 3: 39
Jenkins, Charles Francis *3:* 270
Jenny airmail stamps *1:* 189 (ill.)
Jersey (material) *2:* 256
Jet engine *2:* 131–141, 131 (ill.), 133
(ill.), 134 (ill.), 135 (ill.), 136 (ill.),
140 (ill.)
Jet engine manufacturing *2:* 137 (ill.),
138 (ill.), 139 (ill.)
Joyner, Fred *1:* 230
Judson, Whitcomb L. *1:* 272
Jung, George *2:* 97

K

Kantrowitz, Adrian *3:* 32, 39
Karman, Theodore von *1:* 117
Karp, Haskell *3:* 32
Kellogg, John Harvey *3:* 70
Kellogg's Corn Flakes *3:* 70
Kelly, Charlie *2:* 38, 40
Kelvin, Lord *1:* 239
Keratometers *2:* 67
Ketchup *2:* 161–168, 161 (ill.), 164 (ill.)
Ketchup manufacturing *2:* 162 (ill.),
165 (ill.), 166 (ill.), 167 (ill.)
Kevlar *1:* 48, 51, 173; *2:* 114, 133, 137; *3:*
263
Kevlar production *1:* 51 (ill.)
Kircher, Athanasius *3:* 11
Kodak *2:* 204 (ill.), 205, 206 (ill.), 212
Kolff, Willem *3:* 32
Krazy Kat 3: 12
Krypton *2:* 169

Kumax *1:* 49
Kwolek, Stephanie *1:* 48

L

Laboratory incubator *1:* 206
Lacquer *1:* 262
Laid paper *1:* 184
Landrum, Ed *2:* 214 (ill.)
Lands *1:* 83
Laps. *See* Lens laps
Lappers *2:* 70
Laser cutting *1:* 84
Laser drilling *2:* 137
Laser welding *2:* 6
Lasers *1:* 12, 80, 172; *2:* 6, 32, 70, 107,
123, 127, 137
Lassiter, John *3:* 14
Latex *1:* 247; *2:* 11–17, 50, 57–60, 227
Lathes *2:* 273
Lavassor, Emile *1:* 2
Lawn mower *1:* 137–144, 137 (ill.), 138
(ill.), 141 (ill.), 143 (ill.)
LCD. *See* Liquid crystal display (LCD)
Lead glass *2:* 171
Leap pad *1:* 94
Leather *1:* 191; *2:* 20–22, 24, 25, 41, 102,
111, 114, 194
Leather jacket *3:* **153–161,** 153 (ill.),
155 (ill.), 160 (ill.)
Leather jacket assembly *3:* 159 (ill.)
Leather jacket design *3:* 158 (ill.)
Left ventricular assist device (LVAD)
3: 30, 32, 35
Legumes *2:* 178
Lenoir, Etienne *1:* 2
Lenses *1:* 14
Lens laps *1:* 94
Lensometers *1:* 93, 95 (ill.)
Leonardo da Vinci *1:* 116; *2:* 36
Letterpress *1:* 42
Light bulb *1:* 145–153, 145 (ill.), 148
(ill.), 152 (ill.); *2:* 176, 266
Light bulb manufacturing *1:* 151 (ill.)
Light detection system *1:* 14
Light-emitting diode (LED) *1:* 240, 267
Light-sensitive paper *1:* 210
Lindbergh, Charles *3:* 61
Linnaeus, Carolus *1:* 65

Italic type indicates Series number; **boldface** type indicates main entries featured in Series 3;
(ill.) indicates photographs and illustrations.

INDEX **xvii**

Italic type indicates Series number; **boldface** type indicates main entries featured in Series 3; (ill.) indicates photographs and illustrations.

INDEX **xix**

Perinet, Francois *1:* 257
Perkin, William *2:* 195
Perlman, Itzhak *2:* 287, 288 (ill.)
Permanent hair color *3:* 145
Perry, Thomas *2:* 226
Persians *1:* 46
"Persistence of vision" *3:* 274
PET. *See* Polyethylene terephthalate (PET)
Peter, Daniel *1:* 66; *3:* 163
Petroleum-based products *1:* 2
Petronas Twin Towers *3:* 235, 236 (ill.), 244
Pharmacist *3:* 24 (ill.)
Phenakistoscope *3:* 12
Philately *1:* 185
Phonographs *1:* 80
Phosphor tagging *1:* 183
Photo sensors *1:* 84
Photodetectors *1:* 14
Photodiodes *1:* 14
Photoelectric smoke detectors *2:* 233
Photograph *3:* **204–213,** 204 (ill.)
Photograph development *3:* 209, 210 (ill.)
Photograph manufacturing *3:* 211–212
Photograph materials *3:* 207–209
Photographic film *2:* 202–212, 202 (ill.), 203 (ill.), 206 (ill.)
Photographic film manufacturing *2:* 208 (ill.), 209 (ill.)
Photography *2:* 202–205, 207, 212
Photometers *2:* 181
Photoresist *1:* 84
Photosynthesis *1:* 220
Piano. *See* Player piano
Piano action *2:* 213
Picasso, Paloma *1:* 156
Pierce, John R. *3:* 226
Pietz, John *2:* 1
Piezoelectricity *1:* 266
Pigments *1:* 155, 166; *2:* 12, 13, 14, 188, 191, 227, 237, 254, 286
Pigskin *3:* 118
Pills *1:* 21
Pipeline *3:* 140
Pitch *1:* 260
Pits *1:* 83
Pixels *1:* 106
Pixilation *3:* 13
Planktons *3:* 132

Plantain trees *1:* 63
Plasma *1:* 140
Plasma screen *3:* 276
Plastic creep *2:* 244
Plasticizers *1:* 164
Plateau, Joseph *3:* 12
Plating *1:* 75, 76
Player piano *2:* 213–224, 213 (ill.), 214 (ill.), 219 (ill.), 223 (ill.)
Player piano (disc-driven) *2:* 217 (ill.), 220 (ill.)
Playstation *3:* 285 (ill.)
Plimpton, James *2:* 111
Plucking *1:* 107
Point size *1:* 39
Point-of-sale scanners *1:* 12
Polaroid film *2:* 207, 210
Polishing *1:* 94
Polycarbonate *1:* 91, 93
Polycarbonate sheeting *1:* 121
Polyester *2:* 12, 241, 247, 256
Polyethylene *1:* 173; *2:* 59, 241, 243, 247
Polyethylene terephthalate (PET) *2:* 184, 241–245, 247
Polymers *1:* 230, 247; *2:* 65, 68, 72, 73, 114, 242, 243, 245, 247
Polymerization *1:* 50; *2:* 242, 243, 245
Polyurethane *1:* 194; *2:* 114
Polyvinyl chloride (PVC) *1:* 101
Poly-para-phenylene terephthalamide *1:* 48
Pong *3:* 278
Pop-up books *1:* 38
Porcelain *1:* 149
Porsche *1:* 5 (ill.)
Post, Charles William *3:* 71
Post Toasties *3:* 71
Postage stamp *1:* 181–190, 181 (ill.), 182 (ill.), 183 (ill.), 189 (ill.)
Poulsen, Valdemar *1:* 98
Powder metallurgy *2:* 134, 136, 139
Power reel mowers *1:* 139
Pratt & Whitney *2:* 141
Pre-preg ply *1:* 123
Presley, Elvis *1:* 184 (ill.)
Press cakes *1:* 71
Press proofs *1:* 43
Press-Ewing seismographs *1:* 211
Priestley, Joseph *2:* 225; *3:* 247

Italic type indicates Series number; **boldface** type indicates main entries featured in Series 3; (ill.) indicates photographs and illustrations.

INDEX   **xxi**

S

Sabotage *1:* 232

Saddles *1:* 112

Safe *1:* 79 (ill.)

Safety pins *1:* 272

Salsa *1:* 200–206, 200 (ill.), 201 (ill.), 205 (ill.); *2:* 168

Salsa manufacturing *1:* 203 (ill.), 204 (ill.)

Salsa cruda *1:* 200

San Andreas Fault *1:* 217

Sanctorius Sanctorius *1:* 238

Sanforization *1:* 32

Sanitation compounds *1:* 97

Santa Anna, Antonio Lopez de *2:* 58

Sargent, James *1:* 74

Satellite dish *3:* **225–234,** 225 (ill.), 227 (ill.), 231 (ill.)

Satellite dish components *3:* 230 (ill.)

Satellite dish manufacturing *3:* 228–233, 229 (ill.)

Satellite dish materials *3:* 228

SATRA. *See* Shoe and Allied Trades Research Association (SATRA)

Saws *1:* 122

Sax, Adolphe *1:* 258

Scale armor *1:* 47

Scanners *1:* 12

Scanning *3:* 272

Schakowsky, Harvey *2:* 258

Schaud, Jules *3:* 163

Scheele, Carl *3:* 205

Scheinman, Victor *2:* 120

Schott, Gaspar *3:* 11

Schroeder, William *3:* 32

Schueller, Eugene *3:* 145

Schultz, Augustus *3:* 154

Schulze, Johann Henrich *2:* 202; *3:* 204–205

Screw press *1:* 66

Scribes *1:* 36

Scythes *1:* 137

Seasonal Energy Efficiency Ratio (SEER) *3:* 9

Seat belts *2:* 1, 3, 10

Sechaud, Jules *1:* 66

Sedimentation *1:* 224

Seeberger, Charles D. *3:* 108

SEER. *See* Seasonal Energy Efficiency Ratio (SEER)

Seismograph *1:* 207–218, 208 (ill.), 209 (ill.), 216 (ill.)

Seismograph components *1:* 215 (ill.)

Seismometers *1:* 209

Seismoscopes *1:* 207

Selective inking *1:* 186

Semipermanent hair color *3:* 145

Semple, William F. *2:* 58

Serpentine Railway *3:* 215

Sewing machines *1:* 272

Shackle *1:* 75

"Shakey" *2:* 119

Shannon, C. *1:* 81

Shellac *1:* 18; *2:* 286

Shepard, Alan B., Jr. *3:* 58

Shoe and Allied Trades Research Association (SATRA) *1:* 199

Shoemaking *1:* 196

Shrek *3:* 14 (ill.), 15 (ill.)

Shubin, Lester *1:* 49

Sikorsky, Igor *1:* 117

Silica glass *1:* 172

Silicon *1:* 14, 267; *2:* 30, 72, 98

Silkscreening *1:* 242; *2:* 262

Siloxane *2:* 72

Silver *1:* 83; *2:* 87, 92, 202, 203, 205, 207–209, 211, 236, 282

Silver nitrate *2:* 202

Skids *1:* 120

Skyscraper *3:* **235–245,** 235 (ill.)

Skyscraper building frame *3:* 239 (ill.)

Skyscraper construction *3:* 243 (ill.)

Skyscraper foundation *3:* 241 (ill.)

Skyscraper ground floor *3:* 239 (ill.)

Sloane, Hans *1:* 65

Smoke detector *2:* 233–240, 233 (ill.), 234 (ill.), 235 (ill.)

Smoke detector assembly *2:* 239 (ill.)

Smoke detector components *2:* 238 (ill.)

"Snoopy cap" *3:* 262

Soda bottle *2:* 241–247, 251 (ill.), 245 (ill.), 246 (ill.)

Soda bottle manufacturing *2:* 243 (ill.), 244 (ill.)

Soda dispenser *3:* 250 (ill.)

Soda jerk *3:* 248 (ill.)

Soda machine *3:* 254 (ill.)

Soda water *3:* 247

Italic type indicates Series number; **boldface** type indicates main entries featured in Series 3; (ill.) indicates photographs and illustrations.

INDEX **xxiii**

Italic type indicates Series number; **boldface** type indicates main entries featured in Series 3; (ill.) indicates photographs and illustrations.

INDEX **XXV**